I0448016

ACTUAL FACTS AND FIGURES

OKECHUKWU MARTINS ONUOHA

Actual Facts And Figures

ISBN: 1502519909
ISBN-13: 978-1502519900

DEDICATION

I dedicate this book to Almighty Jehovah.

CONTENTS

Acknowledgments 5

1 Safety Facts Pg 6

2 Logical Facts Pg 22

3 Health Facts Pg 27

4 Social Facts Pg 53

5 Environmental Facts Pg 77

6 Animal And Plant Facts Pg 87

ACKNOWLEDGMENTS

I acknowledge my wife Prisca Chiemeka Martins, my children Somto Frances Martins and Genevieve Dumebi Martins for their love. I thank also my parents Emmanuel and Emelda Onuoha for their parental care over me.

1 SAFETY FACTS

Fact- Did you know - People say 'bless you' when you sneeze, because when you
sneeze, your heart stops for a millisecond!

Fact- Never holds your nose and covers your mouth when sneezing, as it can blow out your eyeballs.

Facts- 55% of people yawn within 5 minutes of seeing someone else yawn. Reading about yawning makes most people yawn. How are you feeling at the moment?

Health- Smoking weakens your heart and shortens your lifespan! So if you want to live longer, quit Smoking!

Fact- Chocolate kills Dogs! It affects a Dogs heart and nervous system; a few ounces are enough to kill a small dog.

Health- Water helps in correct functioning of the kidneys and bowels. At least6-8 glasses of plain water should be drunk each day.

Fact- A normal person will die of total lack of sleep sooner than from starvation. So, go and take a quick nap!

Health- Coconut water is an all natural health drink that can add years to your life.

Health- When battery is down to the last grid/bar, do not answer the phone. The radiation is 1000times more, which can harm you.

Health- Always answer the phone by your left ear. The rays coming out from the mobile phone spoils the brain, if you use the right ear!

Health- 1-2 bananas a day will not only help to gain weight, but will also be effective against skin rashes, digestive disorders and even asthma.

Fact- If you sneeze too hard, you can fracture a rib. If you try to suppress a sneeze, you can rupture a blood vessel in your head or neck and die!

Fact- Were you aware, that wearing headphones for just an hour increases the bacteria in your ear by 700 times.

Fact- What do bullet proof vests, fire escapes, windshield wipers and laser printers have in common? All were invented by women!

Fact-A woman's arthritic pains will almost disappear as soon as she becomes pregnant.

Fact- Amazing! If an identical twin grows up without having a certain tooth, the other twin will most likely also grow up with that tooth missing.
Fact- Laughing can lower the level of stress hormones and strengthen the immune system.

Fact- It's impossible to tickle yourself, because the cerebellum (a part of the brain) warns the rest of the brain that you're about to tickle your self.

Health - Stay away from fried foods that fuel the flames of heartburn and indigestion. Also take time to eat slowly and chew your food thoroughly.

Health- Consume lots of warm water. Consumption of lots of warm water not only burns the calories but also increases the metabolic activity.

Health - Go for a walk after eating. Walk through a park. You will burn calories and get your exercise at the same time!

Health- Regular exercise improves the efficiency of the heart and other body parts and we live longer. Without daily exercise body becomes weak and lazy.

Health- Consumption of excessive alcohol can lead to high blood pressure, obesity, irregular heartbeats, which in turn lead to heart attack.

Health- It is advised to drink more water in the morning and less at night.

Facts- The reason why Tattoos don't vanish even though we shed our skin is because the dye is injected deeper into the dermis part of the skin.

Fact- Not even sunglasses fully protect your eyes from the sun's dangerous ultraviolet (UV) rays. UV can burn your eyes & make you blind!

Fact- Every time one sneezes some of the brain cells die.

Fact- If you fart consistently for 6 years and 9 months, enough gas is produced to create the energy of an atomic bomb.

Fact-The Ebola virus kills 4 out of every 5 humans it infects. Ebola outbreak of 2014 has killed over 3000 people.

Fact- When you are looking at someone you love, your pupils dilate and they do the same when you are looking at someone you hate.

Fact – Our eyes are always the same size from birth, but our nose and ears never stop growing. SCARY!

Fact- You burn more calories sleeping than you do watching television.

Fact- Thirty five percent of the people who use personal ads for dating are already married.

Fact-On average, 100 people choke to death on ball-point pens every year.

Fact- The average computer user blinks 7 times a minute, less than half the normal rate of 20.
Fact-An electric eel can produce a shock of up to 650 volts.

Fact- Colgate faced big obstacles in marketing toothpaste in Spanish speaking countries. That's because when translated, Colgate means 'go hang your-self'.

Fact- The chance of getting a cavity is higher if a candy is eaten slowly throughout the day as compared to eating it all at once & then brushing.

Fact- A moderately severe sunburn damages the blood vessels to such an extent that it takes 4-15 minutes for them to return to the normal condition.

Fact- Did you know? Men without hair on their chests are more likely to get cirrhosis of the liver than men with hair.

Fact- Three Hundred Cells die in your body every minute. Strange!

Fact- Peanuts are one of the ingredients of dynamite.

Fact- One can survive without food but not without sleep. Strange!

Health- To avoid heat Exhaustion: Don't suddenly go out into the sun from an air conditioned room or do the opposite. Learn to acclimatize slowly.

Health- Rub the palms of your hands together vigorously to create heat, then quickly place them over each closed eye and relax for a full minute.

Health- Maintain a regular sleep routine; avoid large meals just before sleeping & get regular exercise but avoid exercising before sleeping.

Health- To keep yourself energetic during work hours, keep your back straight. This might not be possible always, but keep trying & you can do it.

Health- To cure hangover, take banana milkshake, sweetened with honey. Banana calms the stomach & honey builds up tired blood sugar level.

Health- To reduce eyestrain re-focuses your eyes. Look away from your computer screen every 10-15 minutes and focus for 5-10 seconds on a distant object.

Health- Remember the shadow rule: If your shadow is longer than you are tall, you are safe in the sun; if it's shorter than you are, you can burn.

Health- Reduce the chances of having another heart attack by taking capsules that supply a total of 900 mg of omega-3 fatty acids per day.

Health- Replace lost fluids and replenish electrolytes by drinking sports drinks or other re-hydration formulas, or eating vegetable soup.

Health - Use a tooth-paste or mouthwash containing zinc compounds or stabilized chlorine dioxide to help break down odor-causing sulphur chemicals.

Health- Keep your environment free of irritants and allergens that can trigger sinus congestion, such as dust, mould, smoke, chemical fumes.

Health- Control mouth bacteria that cause ear infections by chewing gum or eating candy sweetened with xylitol, a natural sugar found in fruit.

Health- To improve health and reduce alcohol cravings, eat more whole grains, fruit, and other healthful foods, limit sugar, caffeine, and junk food.

Health- If you suffer from cold sores, avoid exposure to sunlight. Wear a lip balm with sun protection and carry a cream with you to treat cold sores.

Health- Tongue should be scraped regularly otherwise it gives rise to foul smells. Scrapers made of copper, steel or plastic can be used.

Health- A gentle massage with warm olive oil is very effective to relieve arthritis pain.

Health- Consume milk and honey daily in the morning for a smooth glowing skin.

Health- A product labeled with a fat-free claim doesn't mean that it is low in calories. Always read the nutrition label on the packaging.

Health- There is no need to avoid starches like potatoes, rice and pasta after your workout when your body is in need of instant energy.

Health- In summer season, eat more fruits and vegetables. This is because they have fairly high water content and good salt balance.

Health - Love your family and other people. In return you will get their love which will make you emotionally strong and healthy.

Health- Improve your chances for long-term weight loss by joining a group while you adjust to new diet and exercise habits.

Fact- Studies have shown that the scent of Rosemary can help in better mental performance and makes individuals feel more alert.

Health- Spinach is a rich source of vitamin A, which has a key role in protecting and maintaining the health of your eyes.

Health- Split your desert with your companion. You will only have to exercise half as long to burn off the extra calories!

Health- It is better to discipline your dietary habits and keep your stomach light. Always eat lesser than your hunger.

Health- It is important to get eight hours of sleep. You will get feel revitalized and this will reflect in your eyes.

Health - Have your soup first. It will help to fill you up and most soups have fewer calories.

Fact- To scare rivals, a male hooded seal blows air into it's nose. This inflates the lining of 1 of its nostrils and it looks like a big red balloon.

Health- Exercise you truly enjoy is much easier to stick to, so find activities that fit your personal style, fitness level and workout opportunities.

Fact- After a certain period of growth, hair becomes dormant. That is, they remain attached to the hair follicle until replaced by new hair.

Health- Cut down on fat when you treat yourself to a Pizza, avoid the luxury of the extra layer of cheese or mayonnaise. Eliminate the cream from salads.

Health - Choose brown rice over white rice, whole grain breads and rolls over white. Not only are they lower in calories but they are better for you.

Health- Increasing protein intake can make the diet highly acidic. To offset this condition, be sure to include more green leafy vegetables in diet.

Health- Having fun is good for relaxing and strengthening the healing power of the body and mind. Do what you like and forget everything else for some time.

Health- Protect your heart by cutting meat and foods containing trans fats; fuel up with nuts, olive oil, fish & other sources of healthy fats instead.

Health- Don't take soft drinks or energy drinks while you are exercising. Stay properly hydrated by drinking enough water during your workout.

Health- Do not skip meals. Many healthy eaters diet by day and binge by night. You are only fooling yourself.

Health- Cut back or eliminate high calorie drinks such as soda, sweet tea and lemonade. If you drink a 20-oz of soft drink everyday, switch to the diet version.

Health - Avoid the super size bagels. Some have a calorie content of 400 -500 calories/bagel. Read the Serving size on the nutrition facts panel.

Health- All energy bars and fruit smoothies are not low in calories. Start to read and compare serving sizes and calorie content.

Health- Your cravings will disappear after 10 minutes if you turn your attention elsewhere. Be careful of snacking.

Health- Avoid suffering from dehydration in summers by drinking more water and eating papaya every day. Oranges and drinking butter milk daily also help.

Health- To get rid of the menstrual cramps, use a good quality heating pad and place it properly on the abdomen or lower back.

Facts- An average human being can live for about 11 days without water.

Health - Eat breakfast, lunch and dinner. If you miss one of these meals, there is a high chance that you will struggle with night time eating and binging.

Health- Eat without engaging in any other simultaneous activity. No reading, watching TV, or sitting at your computer.

Health- Swimming is the most asthma-friendly sport of all, but cycling, canoeing, fishing, sailing and walking is also good, according to the experts.

Health- Aerobics is a great way to keep the heart pacing properly, where walking is most advisable. Try and use the stairs wherever you need to use the lift.

Health- Don't forget to wear your sunglasses whenever you are stepping out. These will protect your eyes from the sun's harmful UV rays.

Health- In case you suffer from asthma, don't forget to take your inhaler or other medication with you whenever you go out.

Health- Always check for the expiry date while purchasing medicines over the counter. Refrain from self-medication and take only what the doctor prescribes.

Health- Don't overlook to take care of your teeth and gums! With the oral cavity, you can get parasites; yeast and fungus get into the body!

Health - Listen to your body. If you find that you are dragging, eat the right foods like carrots, rice, bananas and potatoes. These give instant energy.

Health- Using heat therapy is a great way to reduce long – term effects or injury for overworked muscles.

Health- To get your abdomen in better shape, do ten crunches everyday!

Health- If you have VCR or DVD, try sticking in some good workout tapes. Even taking 15 minutes every day to workout will get you started.

Health- The best way to cure acidity is to drink a glass of water along with a piece of jaggery dissolved in it, after meals.

Health- If not already done, add cabbage to your diet as cabbage cuts out the risk of cancer, especially breast, lung, colon and prostate cancers.

Health- Olive oil reduces the chances of cholesterol level. The presence of alpha-tocopherol in the oil helps in preventing blood arteries disorder.

Health- To prevent weight gain, avoid sweetened soft drinks and fruit juices in favor of water or artificially sweetened drinks.

Health- Don't use headphones or earphones for a long period of time. Rest your ear a while after every hour!

Health- Maintain a balance between your work and health. Don't let stress kill you rather kill the stress by dealing with it smartly.

Health- Drinking water is good for health but excessive drinking may lead to cause strain on your kidneys.

Health- Always take out time to relax. Getting overtired can deplete your immune system leaving you open to infections.

Health- Reduce the intake of salt, sugar and amplified fat in meals. It will keep you away from high blood pressure or any heart disorders.

Health- Banana shake with honey helps in treating hangover as banana calms the stomach and honey helps in building up the tired blood sugar level.

Health- In case of asthma, don't forget to take your inhaler or other medication with you whenever you go out.

Health- Do exercise regularly that opens and lengthens your body rather than repetitive movements that contract and constrict your muscles.

Health- Keep tissues handy for coughs and sneezes and dispose them in a no-touch container. This helps to prevent spreading contagious diseases.

Health- One must eat 5 or more fruits and vegetables daily as these are proven to be strong weapons to fight the forces of flu and colds.

Health- Always wash your hands to keep germs at bay. Viruses and bacteria can live for hours on surfaces touched by an infected person.

Health- It is recommended, never to skip your breakfast, it is the most important meal of the day. It helps in revitalizing your body!

Health - Practice yoga in your daily regime. It is an integrated system for the benefit of the body, mind and inner spirit.

Health- Avoid using your computer just before going to bed as the bright screen light makes your brain think its daytime and drives sleep away.

Health- When you sit in your office chair, rest your feet flat on the floor and keep your thighs parallel to the ground to avoid low back strain.

Health - When dining out, eat only half and take the remainder home. A typical restaurant entrée has 1,000 to 2,000 calories.

Health- It has been observed that a regular intake of chocolate, fruits, vegetables, red wine and tea help you against Alzheimer's disease.

Health- Nail biters beware! The flu virus enters the body through the nose, eyes and mouth. This is a good time to break the habit.

Health- For minor burns first aid, pour cool water for 5 minutes and loosely wrap in gauze. Do not apply ice, oil, butter or ointment.

Health- Eat breakfast everyday and choose steaming over frying or baking to have a healthy heart.

Health- Get a massage regularly. It feels bloody good and promotes circulation and immune system function.

Health - Massage your face with ghee, almond oil or coconut oil before going to bed to avoid premature ageing.

Health- To have a healthy heart, it is best to reduce your complex carbohydrate intake. Instead have protein rich diet!

Fact- Do you know that seatbelts first became mandatory in 1984? Surprising!

Health- To kill stress, always take out time for exercise! Morning walks, jogging, cycling or climb stairs keep you in a good shape!

Health- To have a healthy body at least sleep of 8 hours is needed. It helps in keeping you fresh through out the day.

Fact- The venom of the king cobra is so deadly that just one gram of it can kill 150 people.

Health- Stress destroys the body, so create a balance between your work and your personal life.   Deal with the stress smartly to avoid health risks.

Health- Avoid drinking large amounts of water while eating your meal as it dilutes and hinders the digestion process.

Fact- A mere 2 percent drop down in body water can trigger short-term memory, trouble with basic math and difficulty focusing on the computer screen.

Health- Precautions like washing hands regularly and covering mouth while sneezing are some of the ways to minimize the risk of illnesses.

Health- Increasing your intake of fresh fruits and green leafy vegetables makes your teeth and gums less susceptible to dental decay and erosion.

Health- Diabetic patients must not take honey. Cinnamon too must be taken only in winters because it produces heat in the body.

Health - Avoid reading while lying down and maintain a distance of about 1 to 1.5ft between eyes and your book.

Fact- Diabetes care- Check your feet every day for blisters, cuts, sores, redness or swelling, and treat them right away, if you have diabetes.

Health- Synthetic Sweeteners like Aspartame and Acesulfame – K are widely used in soft drinks, candies, chewing gum etc. Aspartame can cause brain tumours.

Health- Diabetes care- Aspirin reduces your bloods ability to clot. Taking a daily aspirin can reduce your risk of heart attack and stroke.

Health- Best home remedy for high BP is honey mixed with water early in the morning. It is a good medicine that reduces BP levels of the body.

Health- Smokers who have diabetes are three times more likely to die of cardiovascular disease than are non-smokers who have diabetes.

Health- Do you know that the so-called energy sports drinks are chock full of sugar and caffeine? Avoid them as far as possible.

Health- Diabetes care: - consult your Doctor if you have like or other foot problem that does not start to heal with the oceanic?

Health- Drink water even if you are not thirsty as thirst is a poor indicator of how much fluid you need to replace.

Health - Lift up any fallen object by bending at knees, instead of bending back.

Health- If your eye twitches or gets red and you feel itchy, massage your scalp with curd.

Fact- More than 90 percent of plane crashes have survivors.

Health- Eat loads of fresh fruits and green vegetables, as a part of your daily diet. And keep away from processed foods.

Fact- Less than 2 percent of the water on Earth is fresh.

Health- Hiccups Remedy- Try breathing slowly into a paper bag or cup your hands around nose and mouth, and breathe normally.

Health- Do not expect to totally revamp your eating habits overnight. Changing too much, too fast can get in the way of success.

Health- Inhaling the scent of rosemary oil can help you make more alert and attentive. Students can use it during exams to increase their concentration.

Health- If you use birth control pills, use sunscreen SPF 30 because you may be at a higher risk darkening of skin around forehead and mouth.

Health- If blisters develop under a burned skin area, leave them alone. It's actually protecting the skin from further damage and infection.

Fact- Did you know? Modern jet engines are designed to withstand bird strikes, which could snap off engines fan blades and cause a crash.

Health- People with high blood sugar should take good care of their feet. Wash them daily in lukewarm water. Dry gently, especially between toes.

Health- To improve your eating habits, find out what's wrong with them. Write down everything you eat for 3 days. Then check your list!

Health- If you get burnt by the sun, calamine lotion or yoghurt can help cool your skin, or take a cool bath or shower.

Fact- Eating chocolate 3 times a month helps people live longer as opposed to people who over eat chocolate or do not eat chocolate at all.

Health- Prior to sleeping, do not forget to remove contact lenses because lens irritation and drying also cause puffiness.

Health- If you want to be fit then it is essential for you to stop smoking, because it hinders the circulation in the feet.

Health- Go for morning walk by having 2-3 glasses of warm water. This will prevent constipation.

Health- While having cold, avoid foods that are difficult to digest like cheese, milk, oily and spicy foods as well as sweets.

Health- During malaria fever, do not take cold foods in the diet like cucumber, orange, papaya, bananas, watermelons etc.

Health- To keep kidney stones under control, drink plenty of water. Fruit juice is also good for those suffering with kidney stones.

Health- Ascorbic acid in quantity of 6-10 grams when taken for 5-10 days helps to prevent miscarriage.

Health- Lack of water in body would slow you down. Reducing ability to act, making you tired. So, have at least 2 litres of water daily.

Fact- Do you know that in an emergency even coconut water can be used as a substitute for blood plasma. It is sterile and has an ideal pH level.

Health- Keep 1 litre water bottle on your desk at work, remember, water keeps your body hydrated, so drink even when you are not thirsty.

Health- Skin cancer can be prevented by spending less time in hot scorching sun; wearing sun glasses and covered clothes help too.

Health- One should avoid non-vegetarian diet, especially red meat. Eating a non-vegetarian diet can worsen the case of kidney stones.

Health- To protect your heart from diseases, eat onions. Onions are a top source of cardio protective elements called flavonoids.

Health- Relaxing for at least 20 minutes a day will go a long way to reduce blood pressure and your reactions to stress.

Health- Children whose parents smoke are at a higher risk of pneumonia and bronchitis. So avoid smoking in front of your kids!

Health- It is important to get eight hours of sleep. You will feel revitalized and this will reflect in your eyes.

Health- The best diet tip! Change your eating habits! Weight loss diets don't work.

Health- Excessive work and anxiety worsen the case of low blood pressure. Hence, it is better to avoid unnecessary arguments and debates.

Health- If you suffer from cold sores, avoid exposure to sunlight.

Wear a lip balm with sun protection and carry a cream with you to treat cold sores.

Fact- The pilot with the most flying hours is John Edward Long. From 1933-1977, he flew 62,654 hours, achieving a total of more than 7 years airborne.

Health- Do not jog on uneven ground, such as a broken footpath or a stony area.

2 LOGICAL FACTS

Fact- If you take any number between 1 & 9 and multiply it by 9, the sum of the resulting digits will always be 9(ex: 7*9=63; 6+3=9).

Fact- Guinness Book of Records holds the records for being the book most often stolen from Public Libraries.

Fact- The record for the most Olympic medals ever won is held by American swimmer Michael Phelps with 19 medals, 15 of which is Gold thus surpassing Soviet gymnast Larissa Latynina who won 18 medals.

Fact- If you part your hair on the right, you were born to be a carnivorous. If you part it on the left, your physical & psychological make-up is that of a vegetarian.

Fact- Babies cry but they do not produce tears until one to three months after birth.

Fact- One of the most dangerous insect in the world is the common housefly. They carry and transmit more diseases than any other animal in the world.

Fact- The eyes receive approximately 90 percent of all our information, making us basically visual creatures.

Health- Find an outlet for your anger, whether its meditation, sports, or using your pillow as a punching bag.

Fact- The fastest growing tissue in the human body is hair.

Health- Drink plenty of fluids to keep your body hydrated, and to replace the lost by the sunburn in summers.

Health- Heavy food should not be taken at night. The proper time of night meal is 2-3 hours before going to bed.

Fact- The strongest muscle in the body is the tongue!

Fact- There is about 6,800 languages in the world.

Fact- There are about 5,400,000 words in the English language and growing.

Fact- Vitamin K is what is required for clotting of blood.

Fact- USA bought Alaska from Russia for 2 cents an acre.

Fact- The word MAP comes from the Latin word, mappa, and means napkin, cloth, or sheet.

Fact- There is a place called Hell in Michigan. It is about 50 miles from Detroit, Michigan.

Fact- Under the rule of Queen Elizabeth 1, England became one of the most powerful nations in the world.

Fact- Owl is the only bird, which can rotate its head to 270 degrees.

Fact- Women shoplift more often than men; the statistics are 4 to 1.

Health- Laughter is the best medicine according to many doctors. In fact, a single laugh may boost your immune system defence for up to 3 days.

Fact- Should there be a crash, Prince Charles and Prince William never travel on the same airplane as a precaution.

Fact- Like finger prints, everyone's tongue print is different.

Fact- Solid carbon dioxide is called dry ice, because when it melts it does not change into liquid but vaporizes directly.

Fact- Months that begin on a Sunday will always have a Friday the 13th.

Fact- Question- This is the only food that doesn't spoil. What is this? Answer. – Honey.

Fact- Kissing helps prevent tooth decay.

Fact- Leonardo Da Vinci invented the scissors.

Fact- Nerve cells can travel as fast as 120 metres per second.

Fact- One out of 20 people has an extra rib.

Health- Let the dancer in you come alive today, close the door, turn on your music system to highest possible volume and dance like MJ or Madonna.

Fact- Moderate dancing burns 250 to 300 calories an hour.

Fact- Do you know that a bird's heart beats 400 times per minute while resting and up to 1000 beats per minute while flying?

Fact- Men leave their hotel rooms cleaner than women do.

Fact- Did you know? Ice breakers are ships that can break through thick ice. They help to keep routes open for other ships in the winter.

Fact- Did you know? Ice breakers are ships that can break through thick ice. They help to keep routes open for other ships in the winter.

Health- Indoor plants reduce components of air pollution in a room. They also remove CO2, which is correlated with lower work performance.

Fact- Stewardesses is the longest word typed with only the left hand.

Health- Prevent body odour! Always wear washed undergarments. Body odour always lingers on clothes.

Fact- Taphephobia is the fear of being buried alive.

Fact- TCDD is a man-made chemical which is 150,000 time more deadly than cyanide.

Fact- Do you know? The right lung of a human is larger than the left one. This is because of the space and placement of the heart.

Health - Try drinking carrot juice for a period of 3 weeks. This helps in preventing wrinkles and shows amazing results after 2-3 weeks.

Fact- Amazing! If an identical twin grows up without having a certain tooth, the other twin will most likely also grow up with that tooth missing.

Fact- All US presidents have worn glasses. Some just did not like being seen wearing them in public.

Health- Exercise you truly enjoy is much easier to stick to, so find activities that fit your personal style, fitness level and workout opportunities.

Health- We need to work hard to achieve our goals. It will streamline the functioning of our body and mind hence improving the immune system of our body.

Health- If you have had depression, you know how hopeless you can feel. Exercise, changing your diet and even playing with a pet can help improve your mood.

Fact- Paper money is not made from wood pulp but from cotton. This means that it will not disintegrate as fast if it is put in the laundry.

Fact- The chance of being born on Leap Day is about 684 out of a million. Less than 5 million people have their birthday on Leap Day.

Health- Spinach is known to be an anti-aging vegetable and reverses age related breakdowns, making you look youthful and fresh.

Fact- The roar that we hear when we place a seashell next to our ear is not the ocean, but sound of blood surging through the veins in the ear.

Fact- The shortest scheduled airline flight is made between the island of Westray to Papa Westray off Scotland. The flight lasts 2 minutes.

Fact- The verb cleave is the only English word with two synonyms which are antonyms of each other: adhere and separate.

Fact- 65 per cent of those with autism are left handed.

Fact- About 10 percent of the world's population is left-handed.

Health- Tongue should be scraped regularly otherwise it gives rise to foul smells. Scrapers made of copper, steel or plastic can be used.

Fact- An average human being can live for about 11 days without water.

Fact- 'One thousand' contains the letter A but none of the words from 'one' to
'nine hundred ninety-nine' has an A.

3 HEALTH FACTS

Fact- Shingles, a virus infection which causes itching, pains and leaves a spot on the scalp of chicken pox sufferers, is best treated with Apple Cider Vinegar and Cayenne pepper.

Fact- Intelligent people have more zinc and copper in their hair.

Fact- Humans have 46 chromosomes, peas have 14 and crayfish have 200.

Fact- DNA was first discovered in 1869 by Swiss Friedrich Mieschler.

Health- Mushrooms are rich in copper. A single serving of mushrooms is said to provide about 20-40 percent of one's daily need of copper.

Health- Spinach is known to be an anti-aging vegetable and reverses age related breakdowns, making you look youthful and fresh.

Health- Both jogging and walking are great ways to get fit. They tone the muscles, relieve stress create a healthier heart and improve lung capability.

Health- Fish is a good source of omega 3 that prevents heart from cholesterol. So, having fish in the meal is a good option.

Fact- The botanical name of the chocolate plant is Theobramba cacao, which means Food of the gods.

Health- Have Almonds as they contain as much protein per ounce as red meat. Also, they aid in reducing the risk of heart attacks by up to 50 percent.

Health- Use onions for curing infections, burns, bee stings and itch of athletes foot as it contains mild antibiotic properties.

Health- The best time for you to sleep is between 10pm at night to 6am in the morning. It keeps you fit and fine.

Facts- Are you afraid of vegetables? If yes then you may be suffering from Lachanophobia! It's the fear from vegetables.

Fact- A woman's sense of smell is most sensitive during ovulation.

Fact- Brains are more active in sleeping than watching TV.

Fact- The muscle that lets your eye blink is the fastest muscle in your body; it allows you to blink 5 times in a second. Women blink twice as much as
men.

Fact-It's so surprising! Human saliva has a boiling point that is three times that of regular water.

Fact-It has been proved that apples are more effective than caffeine at keeping people awake at night.

Fact- A human heart is just 10 ounces and beats nearly 1,000,000 times per
day. It pumps about a cupful of blood every time it beats.
Fact- A human heart can create enough pressure that can squirt blood at a
distance of 30ft. In a lifetime, the heart pumps about 1 million barrels of
blood.

Fact-Approximately two-thirds of a person's body weight is water. Blood is 92% water, the brain is 75% water and the muscles are 75% water.

Fact-Human tonsils can bounce higher than a rubber ball of similar weight and size but only till the first 30 minutes of them being removed.

Fact-Human hair grows about half an inch per month. They grow faster in the summer than in winters.

Fact- Shockingly, if humans go blind in one eye, they only lose about one fifth of their vision but fully lose their sense of depth.

Fact-Shocking! An average human body contains enough Iron to make a 3-inch nail and enough sulphur to kill all the fleas on an average dog.

Fact-Do you know, watching an hour of soap operas burns more calories than watching a three-hour baseball game.

Fact- Humans use an average of 43 muscles to frown, whereas to smile, only 17 do the trick. So keep smiling!

Fact- Fingernails grow nearly 4 times faster than toenails.

Fact- The pupil of the human eye expands as much as 45 percent when a person looks at something pleasing.

Fact- Banging your head against a wall uses 150 calories an hour.

Fact- Right-handed people live, on average, nine years longer than left-handed people do.

Fact-There are more living organisms on the skin of each human than there are humans on the surface of the earth.

Fact- An individual blood cell takes about 60 seconds to make a complete circuit of the body.

Fact- The first synthetic human chromosome was constructed by US scientist in 1997.

Fact-Ninety percent of all teenagers suffer from some of acne.

Fact- If left alone, 70% of birth marks gradually fade away.

Fact – There are approximately 550 hairs in the eyebrow.

Fact- We are about 1cm taller in the morning than in the evening. Layers of cartilage in the joints get compressed during the day.

Fact- Only one person in two billion will live to be 116 0r older.

Fact- The liquid inside young coconuts can be used as substitute for blood plasma'.

Fact- A barrel of juice or wine would take about a year or two to ferment naturally into vinegar.

Fact- All the hydrogen atoms in our bodies were created 12 billion years ago in the Big Bang.
Fact- Saccharin is 500 to 700 times sweeter than sugar.

Fact- Did you know that without the lining of mucus, your stomach would digest itself.
Fact- Wilhelm Rontgen won the first Nobel Prize for physics for discovering X-rays in 1895.

Fact- Astronauts cannot belch- there is no gravity to separate liquid from gas in their stomachs.
Fact- Bloodsucking hookworms inhabit 700 million people worldwide.
Fact-The Australian Billy goat Ipum contains 100 times more vitamin C than an orange.
Fact- Human tapeworms can grow up to 22.9m.

Fact- When you blush, the lining of your stomach also turns red.
Fact- Molecularly speaking water is actually much drier than sand.
Fact- It takes about 20 seconds for a red blood cell to circle the whole body.
Fact- The only part of the body that has no blood supply is the cornea in the eye. It takes in oxygen directly from the air.

Fact- Seniors who drink a cup of coffee before a memory test score higher than those who drink a cup of decaffeinated coffee.
Fact- Do you know, about 8 million blood cells die in the human body every second and the same number are born each second.
Fact- The human head is one -quarter of our total length at birth but only one-eight of our total length left by the time we reach adulthood.
Fact- On an average a human being blinks over 20,000,000 times a year.

Fact- It takes approximately 12 hours for food to digest.

Fact- Ketchup was once sold as a patented medicine. In the 1830s it was marketed in the US as Dr. Miles's compound Extract of tomato.

Fact- We loses half a liter of water a day through breathing. This is the water vapor we see when we breathe onto glasses.

Fact- There is more cells in the human body than there are people living on earth.

Fact- Quite surprising but true! In every two seconds, someone in the U.S. needs blood.

Fact- One could remove a large part of his internal organs and survive. Surprising!

Fact- On an average, every human being produces approximately 25,000 quarts of spit in a lifetime.

Health- Honey contains nutraceuticals, which are effective in removing free radicals from our body. So, take honey to improve your body's immunity.

Health - Increase your protein intake. Without protein body can't build new muscle. Protein also helps to increase metabolism, which burns calories.

Health- Instead of eating 3 big meals, small frequent meals help to balance calorie intake throughout the day & keep your blood sugar level balanced.

Health- Adopt the habit of meditating. Doing so twice a day can help save on medical bills. You not only get a better body but a peaceful mind too.

Health- Vitamin B to a great extent influences proper blood circulation. Eggs, soy products, Carrots, cauliflower are good sources of the vitamin.

Fact- A hard working adult sweats up to 4 gallons per day, but most of the sweat evaporates before a person realizes its there.

Fact- The pupil of the human eye expands as much as 45 percent when a person looks at something pleasing. Surprised, are you?

Fact- There is as much hair per square inch on your body as a chimpanzee. You don't see all of them because most are too fine & light to be noticed.

Fact- Were you aware that in a lifetime, an average person produces about 25,000 quarts of saliva, enough to fill two swimming pools!

Fact- When you stop feeling thirsty, that is the time you need to drink even more water as a human body when dehydrated shuts off its thirst mechanism.

Fact- It is hard to believe, that the acid in a human stomach is strong enough to dissolve razor blades.

Fact- It is believed that from all the oxygen that a human breathes, twenty percent goes to the brain.

Health- Prevent & treat anemia with supplemental iron, vitamin B12 & folic acid; you shouldn't take iron unless a blood test has revealed a deficiency.

Health- Aim for total nutrition with a multivitamin; ensure your body is getting the vitamins and minerals it needs to prevent common infections.

Health- Sip green tea or munch on a few nuts to fight bad cholesterol. High blood lipids require a combination of diet & exercise as initial step.

Health-Oats are low in fat & salt; they are a good source of calcium, they are ideal for heart, bones & nails.

Health- Potassium helps normalize the heartbeat, sends oxygen to the brain & regulates body's water balance, so eat potassium rich food as banana.

Health- Close your eyes for a few minutes & think of a very peaceful place, where you were relaxed & happy. When you open your eyes, you will feel refreshed.

Health- To stop tooth decay and any mouth diseases, the best remedy is to sprinkle dry neem-leaves powder on tooth paste when you brush the teeth.

Health- Practicing Yoga makes organs of the body active in their functioning and has good effect on internal functioning of the human body.

Health- Always avoids any fried or oily foods whenever possible. Instead introduce fruits and vegetables in their raw forms to your diet plan.

Health - Try to limit eating fast food as much as possible. Fast food is known to be salty and greasy and has little nutritional value source.

Health- Add a daily dose of exercise to your routine. There is nothing like a morning walk to start with. A walk will recharge you for the whole day.

Health- A diet which is rich in oats may help stabilize blood glucose levels, which could help people with non-insulin dependent diabetes.

Fact- If you are consuming calories more than your body requires then, this is the reason why you are gaining weight. So avoid them and stay fit!

Health- Consider your immune system, daily nutritional requirements and sustaining strength while consuming meals and drinks throughout the day.

Fact- Jacanas are water birds that live in tropical places. Their very long toes allow them to step on water plants without sinking.

Health- You should take a daily multi-vitamin and mineral supplement. Choose one of good quality, an appropriate supplement for your age and gender.

Health- If you have had depression, you know how hopeless you can feel. Exercise, changing your diet and even playing with a pet can help improve your mood.

Health- Consumption of celery has been found to be to be linked with lowering of blood pressure, so it's good for persons suffering from the hypertension.

Health-Coconut oil improves the body ability to absorb important minerals, as calcium and magnesium which are necessary for development of bones.

Health- By adding an apple or a glass of hot milk to your child's breakfast you could protect them from depression, anxiety and disobedience.

Health- Raisins soaked in a glassful of drinking water for at least 24 hours are a great remedy for chronic constipation.   Drink the water as well.

Health - Add just a fruit or vegetable serving daily. When you get comfortable with that, add an extra serving per day until you reach 8-10 servings per day.

Health- A smoothie made with fat-free milk, frozen fruit, and wheat germ (or protein powder) can be a great meal replacement.

Health- Protect your heart by cutting meat and foods containing Trans fats; fuel up with nuts, olive oil, fish & other sources of healthy fats instead.

Health- Constipation that starts suddenly should be evaluated by a healthcare professional to make sure no serious diseases are the cause.

Health- Ensure your child eats a nutritious diet not only to boost immunity system but also to improve the effectiveness of vaccinations.

Health- Eating vitamin C rich foods with meals and taking 100 to 500mg of vitamin C with iron supplements will improve your iron absorption.

Health- Celery helps in the clearing of uric acid from painful joints, it is said to be helpful in treating arthritis and rheumatic problems.

Health- A watermelon is an ideal health food; it is 92% water, doesn't contain any fat & is a great source of vitamin A, B6 & beta-carotene.

Health- Major part of your diet should consist of food rich in nutrients but not calories to keep you full longer without making you fat.

Health- Extra vitamins and minerals will help ensure your body gets the nutrition it needs, especially if you are avoiding certain foods.

Health- Mix olive oil, ginger root and apply it on your scalp before shampooing for dandruff.

Health- Custard Apple or Seethaphal is low in calories and contains minerals like iron, phosphorous, calcium and riboflavin. This fruit promotes digestion.

Health- We need to work hard to achieve our goals. It will streamline the functioning of our body and mind hence improving the immune system of our body.

Health- Good eating habits are a strong foundation to good health. It's important to eat what you like also to experiment with a variety of new foods.

Health- Choose the right diet for you. Find your ideal weight and discover helpful weight loss supplements to keep the pounds off once and for all.

Health- Put dance to music with your family in your home and be active with your kids. It's one of the easiest ways to involve the whole family in exercise.

Health- Carbohydrates with a high glycaemic index, such as bread, sugar, honey and grain-based food will give instant energy and accelerate your metabolism.

Health- Use a salad plate instead of a dinner plate, a desert bowl instead of soup bowl and a juice glass instead of water tumbler.

Health- Relieve eye stress! Look straight ahead at eye level then slowly to the left and then right, maintaining the eye level. Repeat this 3 or 4 times.

Facts- Did you know that humans blink over 10,000,000 times a year!

Health- Think Yoga's too serene to burn calories? Think again. You can burn 250 to 350 calories during an hour-long class.

Health- De-stressing can be a great way to slim down. By doing meditation, yoga, or even writing in a diary for 20 minutes, one can lose an average of 10 pounds.

Health - Spice up your meals. Capsaicin, a compound found in jalapeno and other spicy peppers, increases the body's release of stress hormones and speed up metabolism.

Health- Enjoy bicycling! It exercises the body and builds a stronger cardiovascular system. It also allows getting out and enjoying nature and fresh air.

Health- Eat the low-cal items on your plate first. Start with salads, veggies, and broth soups, and eat meats and starches last.

Health- Berries contain anthocyanidins that are incredible antioxidants and have resveratrol, which helps fight heart disease and cancer.

Health- Dancing is so much fun, its whole idea is to move your body. Dancing has long been recommended as an avenue to fitness.

Health- Tennis is not only a sport, but also a great way to exercise. This is a great way to strengthen the cardiovascular system and lose weight.

Fact- The average person eats almost 1500 pounds of food a year. Quite a big amount, isn't it?

Fact- Oxygen, carbon, hydrogen and nitrogen make up 90 of the human body.

Health - Eat potatoes and grain products. The starch through digestion is converted into sugar, which supplies energy to keep you up for the whole day.

Fact- Shockingly, if humans go blind in one eye, they only loose about one fifth of their vision but fully loose their sense of depth.

Fact- Approximately two thirds of a persons body weight is water. Blood is 92% water, the brain is 75% water and the muscles are 75% water.

Fact- The normal energy used by our brain is 0.1 calories per minute, and could go up to 1.5 during activities such as puzzle-solving.

Health- Opt for having a heavy breakfast, normal lunch and a light dinner. This is the golden rule that is recommended by all nutritionists.

Health- To stay fit and healthy, go for vegetarian meal over non-vegetarian meals. Have meat as a side coarse and not as your main course.

Fact- During the entire lifetime, an average human being eats about 60,000 pounds of food, that's the weight of about 6 elephants.

Health- Maintain the energy level by limiting your intake of fat and sugar; focus on carbohydrates, fruits and vegetables.

Health- Daily food intake should contain, about 15 to 20% is protein, 40 to 50% is complex carbohydrates and 20 to 30% is fat.

Health- Drink every morning a glass of lukewarm water with little honey and lemon on empty stomach. It keeps a check on your weight.

Health- Try to add a tinge of stretching exercises in your daily routine.

It will surely help you in maintaining a fitter body.

Fact- The smallest bone in the human body is the stapes or stirrup bone located in the middle ear. It is approximately 0.11inches (0.28cm) long.

Health- The best way to cure instant back pain is to heat some coconut oil mixed with a little camphor powder and apply on the affected area.

Health- Choose eggs over bagels. They shed the extra pounds because they felt fuller after breakfast and ate fewer calories during the day.

Health- Relieve eye stress! Look straight ahead at eye level then slowly to the left and then right, maintaining the eye level. Repeat this 3 or 4 times.

Health –Is stress getting you down? Then try yoga. It is one of the best stress relieving activities. Fix a suitable time and practice it everyday.

Health- Avoid fatty foods and go for low fat versions of food that will help you to control your body weight.

Health- To make your body flexible, walking is the best and easy exercise. It also maintains the weight of your body.

Fact- Amazing! When you walk down a steep hill, the pressure on your knees is equal to three times your body weight.

Health- When trying to control calories, make each calorie count by choosing healthy foods that you like and avoiding every bite that you won't enjoy.

Health - Choose healthier fruit. Formerly FDA-rated as 80 calories, apples are now 130. Other fruits got a calorie upgrade like Peaches and Oranges.

Health- Your cravings will disappear after 10 minutes if you turn your attention elsewhere. Be careful of snacking.

Health- It is advisable to eat fruits in the morning for your breakfast. Avoid eating fruits right after meals.

Health- Underweight? All measures to put on weight failed? Then add musk melons, mango, raisins and milk in your diet plan and see the difference.

Health- Put some castor plant leaves in warm sesame oil. Now dab this oil around the ears. This is an excellent natural remedy for relieving ear ache.

Health- To provide an immediate relief from headache, take the juice of three slices of lemon and add it to a cup of tea. Drink this for fast relief.

Health- Gargling provides immediate relief from sore throat. Pour 4 teaspoons of salt in a litre of water and gargle with this water after warming it.

Health- For an immediate relief from pain caused by piles, mix white radish juice with honey and apply it directly on the affected area.

Health- Itching can develop at unexpected places. Applying coconut oil over the affected area is one good and effective home remedies to cure itching.

Health- A visit to the doctor on a regular basis should be made a routine. This needs to be done for preventive care and counselling.

Health- Boost energy by eating just 1,500 calories a day, and loose a pound a week with the easy, nutritionist-approved meal plans.

Health- If you do not eat fish, include walnuts, broccoli, and spinach in your diet to get your dose of omega 3 fatty acids.

Health- When eating anything, slow down and chew each mouthful thoroughly for the best digestion and assimilation possible.

Health- If you love to drink milk, then drink raw milk in its purest form for the most benefit.

Health- Eat more nuts and seeds like walnuts, hazelnuts, almonds, pistachios, sunflower seeds and chia seeds!

Health- If you are a diabetic, regularly visit your eye care professional to prevent associated eye problems.

Fact- Surgeons who listen to music during operations perform better than those who don't. Let's gift them a music system!

Health- One must eat 5 or more fruits and vegetables daily as these are proven to be strong weapons to fight the forces of flu and cold.

Health- Looking for a tasty and filling snack that has less than 100 calories? Have a boiled egg as it contains only about 70-80 calories.

Health- Use fresh chopped garlic as often as you can because the packaged and preserved garlic paste loses a lot of its health benefits.

Health- Lime is useful in maintaining the health of the teeth and bones. It prevents decay and loosening of the teeth, caries and bleeding of the gums.

Health- To lighten freckles, mash unripe currants and mix with honey. Put it on freckles and rinse off after 30 minutes and dab on diluted fresh lemon juice.

Fact- Babies are born without knee caps. They don't appear until the child reaches 2 to 6 years of age. That's interesting!

Health- Avocados are very good for health as it supplies you with oleic acid that aids weight loss and helps to stave off hunger pangs.

Health -Take vitamin A and D in the correct ratio. This is roughly 12.5:1, or 5000iu to 400iu. This will help your body absorb the vitamins.

Health- Individuals who suffer from constipation should increase their intake of fibre through the diet such as brown rice and ripe bananas.

Health- Processed foods are loaded with unhealthy E-numbers, artificial sweetener and trans fat which is not good for your health. Avoid these!

Health - Have lentils in your meal as they are packed with the amino acid leucine. It burns fat fast and could see you lose 7 kg in 10 weeks.

Health- Eat an apple 15 minutes before your meal. In this way, you consume 187 fewer calories on an average than usual.

Health- Steam inhalation is an effective home remedy for coughing and headaches that mitigates the intensity of the pain.

Fact- Dry cereal for breakfast was invented by John Henry Kellogg at the turn of the century! Great!

Health- Eat three 250- calorie, high protein snacks per day. This helps in loosing the extra fat present in the body more easily.

Health- Tomatoes suppress the hormone ghrelin which is responsible for hunger pangs thus these are really good for your health.

Health- To prevent discomfort and indigestion after meals, add some lime juice and black pepper to a few pieces of ginger and chew on them after eating.

Health- Sunflower seeds help in lowering high blood cholesterol. The linoleic acid in it helps in reducing cholesterol deposits on the walls of arteries.

Fact- The only joint less bone in your body is the hyoid bone in your throat! Amazing!

Health- Eye infections such as a stye can be relieved by placing a warm compress over the affected eye. This helps to bring down the swelling and redness.

Health- If you are having flu, have Ginger tea as it helps alleviate the symptoms. Use 2 to 3 pieces of ginger to prepare this tea and take it at regular intervals.

Health- The anti-inflammatory properties of turmeric helps in easing the symptoms of cold. It is best to have a hot glass of turmeric and ginger mixed in milk.

Health- Beet roots are very helpful in curing anaemia. It contains all the essential nutrients like potassium, phosphorus, iodine, iron, vitamins B1, B2, B6, etc.

Health- Fat-free isn't healthy, you do need some fat in your diet. There are some essential fatty acids such as omega-3 that should be a regular part of your diet.

Health- Multiply your body weight in pounds by 10 to know how many calories you need to eat. So if you want to slim down to 125 pounds then cut down to 1250 calories.

Health- Add a bit of chilli to your meals. It fires up your metabolism which helps to process fat faster.

Health- Just add a bit of paprika to your meals, the ground red pepper has six times more vitamin C than a tomato.

Health- For dandruff, apply a paste of soaked fenugreek seeds on the scalp and wash it off with cold water.

Health- To have a younger looking skin and to prevent wrinkles, apply pure castor oil on your body daily.

Health- Drink plenty of fluids and oral re-hydration solutions as electrolyte loss and dehydration are the most common cause of muscle cramps.

Health - Use garlic in its raw form to get rid of cold and sinus. Due to its antibacterial and antifungal properties, garlic can offer a lot of relief.

Health- Try to make a tonic with tomato and carrot juice, mixed with honey, as it works wonder for growing children. Try it!

Health- It is always advised to eat more natural and unprocessed foods and to eliminate the processed food from your diet as it keeps a check on your diabetes.

Health- If you want to have good metabolism, toxin free body, beautiful skin then drinking plenty of water as water aids in digestion and muscle recovery.

Health- If you are willing to have healthy nervous system, then include food products that are rich in vitamin B12 such as meat, milk and cereals.

Health - Look for natural remedies before pharmaceutical ones as they have no side effects and are extremely effective.

Health- Eat as early in the evening as possible and leave at least two full hours after eating before going to sleep.

Health- Have pineapple fruit as evening snack. It sparks your metabolism and has bromolina which helps in breaking down protein particles.

Health-Oats are low in fat & salt; they are a good source of calcium, they are ideal for heart, bones & nails.

Fact- After age 30, the brain shrinks a quarter of a percent(0.25percent) in mass each year. Poor brain!

Health- Breathing exercises help to improve breathing capacity and strengthen the lungs. It reduces the effect of wheezing!

Health-Drink a lot of warm fluids but avoid hot coffee or tea. Green tea or soup can help dilute the mucus and relieve the symptoms of a throat obstruction.

Health- Raw potatoes are beneficial in the treatment of warts. They should be cut and rubbed on the affected area several times daily, for at least two weeks.

Health- Bottle gourd is one of the best vegetables for treating tuberculosis. Use of cooked bottle gourd helps in developing immunity against tubercular germs!

Health- Steam inhalation is greatly helpful in soothing inflamed nasal passages. You can add few drops of eucalyptus or peppermint essential oil to the hot water.

Health- Onion juice mixed with honey is a great way to get rid of chest congestion and cough.

Health-Ginger is a remedy for whooping cough. A teaspoonful of fresh ginger juice, mixed with a cup of fenugreek decoction and honey, is a good diaphoretic.

Fact- Did you know that the brain doesn't feel pain! Even though the brain processes pain signals, the brain itself does not actually feel pain.

Health- Dip a small piece of cotton in a bit of white vinegar and plug it into the bleeding nostril. This remedy will help seal up the wall of the blood vessel.

Fact- Can you guess why onion has such a strong smell? Well, Onions get their distinctive smell by soaking up sulphur from the soil!

Health- For the treatment of scurvy in children, give cows milk to them. This will allow the child to receive the required daily allowance of vitamin C.

Health- For tonsillitis, the patient should avoid spices as they tend to irritate the throat. Sour substances and fried foods should also be avoided.

Fact- A human being drinks 16,000 tons of water in a lifetime.

Health-Warm bath is the highly helpful water treatment for joint pains.

Fact- 25 percent of your bones are located in your feet.

Fact- A person at rest generates as much heat as a 100watt light bulb.

Health- Mix 1tbs of juice of seeds of papaya with 10 drops of lime juice and have it 2 times daily for a month. It works well for liver cirrhosis.

Health- Take 2-3 leaves of the guava and a number of catechu. Chew them together. This will heal even the most persistent of ulcers within a few days.

Health- For correct treatment of varicose veins, the patient must be put on a juice fast for 4-5 days in the start or on an all-fruit diet for 7-10 days.

Health- Fruits like oranges, berries, guavas, kiwis and melons are rich in vitamin C which is very helpful in fighting cold and flu.

Health- Honey is notable for building haemoglobin in the body. This is mostly due to the iron, copper, and manganese contained in it.

Health- For kidney pain, include watermelon juice, parsley tea, barley water, mullein tea, and potassium broth and watermelon seed tea.

Fact- The average human head has 100,000 hair follicles, each of which is capable of producing 20 individual hairs during a person's lifetime.

Fact- The best thing that can be done while peeling onions is chewing gum as it will help in reducing your tears.

Health- Aerobic exercise increases insulin sensitivity, when combined with good eating, it can help restore a normal glucose metabolism, benefiting people with diabetes.

Fact- Virus can be found in all forms of life, including humans, animals, plants, fungi and bacteria. They are 20 to 100 times smaller than bacteria.

Fact - About 400 different kinds of microbes live on and in the human body.

Health- Truvada is a USA approved HIV prevention pill.

Health- Choose to stand while talking on phone. In 30 minutes you can burn 58 calories.

Fact - An average human produce 1.43 pints sweat in a day.

Health- Dehydration causes headache, weakness and leaves you tired. You will be surprised at nice pick me up effect you can get from drinking coconut water.

Health- Food containing fibre like beans, nuts, seeds, fruits, whole grains, and vegetables are very good for diabetes as they control blood sugar.

Fact- A sneeze can travel as fast as 100 miles per hour.

Health- Endorphines are the happiness chemicals found in brain, released during exercise, excitement, pains, and consumption of spicy food or orgasm.

Health- Half an hour of swimming burns 360 calories, which is the equivalent of running at 12 kph for the same amount of time.

Fact- The longest living cells in the body are brain cells which can live an entire lifetime.

Health- Before starting an exercise program, consult your doctor if you have any health related issues or if your age is above 40, do so to avoid injuries.

Health- Bicycling, full body crunches and ball crunches are the best exercises for achieving six pack abs and improving your body composition.

Health- As the saying goes, you are what you eat. Diet and nutrition are the most important facets in maintaining a healthy fitness level.

Fact- Bananas contain natural chemical which can make a person happy. This same chemical is found in Prozac.

Health- Before performing the blood glucose test, make sure your hands are clean. Wash your hands with a mild anti-bacterial soap.

Health- Using an antibacterial mouthwash clean your teeth, tongue, gums, mouth and also between the teeth for complete dental care.

Fact-By the age of 60, most people have lost 50 percent of their taste buds.

Health - Drink raw vegetable juices of carrot- 300ml, chukandar-100ml and cucumbers- 100ml for overcoming fatigue.

Health- Fruits and veggies contain salicylic acid, non-steroidal anti inflammatory drug which helps in preventing heart attacks.

Fact- Your ribs move about 5 million times a year, every time you breathe.

Fact- Your stomach has to produce a new layer of mucus every two weeks, otherwise it will digest itself.

Health - Drink ¼-cup onion juice, a tablespoon honey, and 1/8-tablespoon black pepper for relief from Asthma.

Health- Fresh hot lime water can help ease several digestion issues including nausea, heartburn and parasites.

Health- Drinking lemon water helps in loosing weight, especially, in lukewarm water with honey.

Health- Lemon juice reduces phlegm production and thus helps dissolving gallstones.

Health- Most of the heart problems can be overcome with the help of diet rich in vitamin C.

Health- Juice of carrot and tomato, mixed with some honey, is a good tonic for children.

Health- For a good sleep and to wake up fresh, try to eat a light dinner 2 hours before sleeping. Also, avoid coffee, sugar just before bed.

Fact- Nitrous oxide can make you laugh. That is why it is called laughing gas.

Fact- On average, a person has two million sweat glands.

Fact- Lab tests can detect traces of alcohol in urine to 6 to 12 hours after a person has stopped drinking.

Health - Include watermelon in your diet. They are not only low in calories and fat but also loaded with lycopene which is a heart-healthy antioxidant.

Health- Niacin vitamin works wonders in overcoming migraine headache. Rich sources are yeast, tomatoes, green vegetables, nuts, liver and fish.

Health- Mango seeds are of great value for treating leucorrhoea. Apply 1 tablespoon paste of decorticated kernel of mango inside the vagina.

Health- Lemon juice detoxes liver and improves digestion. Daily use of lemon also prevents accumulation of cholesterol in blood vessels.

Health- Lemon water controls high BP, dizziness and nausea. It prevents relaxation to mind and body reducing mental stress and depression.

Health- Vinegar is a natural astringent, it cleanses wound and helps in healing. Dilute vinegar with water then pat it over the open abrasion.

Health- Lemon is very beneficial for asthma. The juice of one lemon, diluted in a glass of water and taken with meals, will bring good results.

Health- Oranges are useful in the treatment of TB. A glass of orange juice with a pinch of salt and honey must be taken daily by the patient.

Health- For high cholesterol level should drink 8-10 glasses of water every day, as water stimulates the excretory activity of the kidneys.

Health- Beal fruit is finest of all laxatives. It cleans and tones up the bowels and thus very useful in the treatment of constipation.

Health- Coconut water is helpful in passing off small stones through urine. It also reduces the toxic substance found in the body.

Health- If suffering from kidney stones, avoid vegetables like cauliflower, peas, carrots etc and fruits like strawberries and parsley.

Health- Olive oil helps preventing wrinkles. It removes the oil from skin, makes your skin soft, and takes away the stress in your face or body.

Health- The jujube leaves helps in curing obesity. A handful of leaves soaked overnight, must be taken in the morning on an empty stomach.

Health- Drinking water kept overnight in a copper container accumulates traces of copper, which is said to build up the muscular system.

Health- To cure arthritis permanently, take 2 tsp of calcium lactate, 3 times each day in water, before meals for at least 4 months.

Health- Bananas, a rich source of vitamin B6, have proved helpful in the treatment of arthritis. The patient may eat 8-9 bananas daily.

Health- Pineapple juice is considered valuable in the treatment of tuberculosis. Drink 1 glass of pineapple juice everyday.

Health- It is said that 5 leaves of holy basil, taken on a daily basis, can help us avoid diseases such as hepatitis and typhoid.

Fact- Do you know, the women who snore are at an increased risk of high blood pressure and cardiovascular disease than men!

Fact- Do you know that Melanin and exposure to ultraviolet light are needed to bring out the true colour of babies eyes else all will have blue eyes.

Health- To reduce body odour mix some rosewater or sandalwood essential oil in your bath-tub and take a bath with this medicated water.

Health- Coconut water is an excellent remedy for gastritis. It gives the stomach necessary rest and provides vitamins and minerals.

Health- Drink a glass of water, prior to every meal. Thirst is sometimes mistaken for hunger. It also helps in decreasing your intake.

Health- To cure bad breath rinse your mouth before sleeping with a glass of water with the juice of half a lemon added to it.

Health- When you feel an anxiety attack coming, you can have a cold shower or soak in a warm bath, whichever works for you.

Health- Vitamin E has been found to reduce cancer risk when consumed at recommended levels. Consult your doctor before taking!

Health- The use of vitamin E oil is valuable in chicken pox. This oil should be rubbed on the skin.

Health- The juice of raw beetroot is one of the most effective remedies for low BP. The patient should drink a cup of this juice twice daily.

Health- Eat an apple a day; it cleanses the body's digestive system by removing toxins and therefore preventing health problems.

Health- Make a habit of maximum walking on foot. This is beneficial not only for your body but for your mind also.

Health- For the initial stage of malaria, be on the orange juice and water diet to enhance the body's immunity system.

Health- Aromatherapy is a good treatment for anxiety. Lavender oil is particularly effective but you can also use jasmine or sandalwood.

Health- Cut back or eliminate high calorie drinks such as soda, sweet tea and lemonade. If you drink a 20-oz of soft drink everyday, switch to the diet version.

Health- Coconut oil improves the body ability to absorb important minerals, as calcium and magnesium which are necessary for development of bones.

Health- Mushrooms are rich in copper. A single serving of mushrooms is said to provide about 20-40 percent of ones daily need of copper.

Fact- The double-helix structure of DNA was discovered in 1953 by James Watson and Francis Crick. The length of a single human DNA is 1.7m.

Health- Prevent and treat anaemia with supplemental iron, vitamin B12 and folic acid; you should not take iron unless a blood test has revealed a deficiency.

Health- Consume lots of warm water. Consumption of lots of warm water not only burns the calories but also increases the metabolic activity.

Health- A watermelon is an ideal health food; it is 92 percent water, does not contain any fat and is a great source of vitamin A, B6 and beta-carotene.

Health- There is no need to avoid starches like potatoes, rice and pasta after your workout when your body is in need of instant energy.

Health- Banana is considered valuable in the treatment of peptic ulcer, as it works towards neutralizing the acidic effects of gastric juices.

Health- To relieve backache problem, consume glucose or honey in warm water in the morning.

Health- Having a good sob is reputed to be good for you. So is laughter, which has been shown to help heal bodies, as well as broken hearts.

4 SOCIAL FACTS

Fact- Typewriter was invented by Hungarian immigrant Qwert Yuiop, who left his 'signature' on the keyboard. See your phone keyboard and computer/laptop keyboard.

Fact-King Henry 1 who ruled England in the 12th century, standardized the 'yard' as the distance from the thumb of his outstretched arm to his nose.

Fact- The shortest war in history was between Zanzibar and England in 1896. Zanzibar surrendered in just 38 minutes.

Fact- Thomas Edison, the inventor of the light bulb, was afraid of the dark.

Fact- There are only four words in the English language which end in '-dous' tremendous, horrendous, stupendous and hazardous. Sounds dangerous!

Fact- Dreamt is the only English word that ends in the letters 'mt'.

Fact- Did you know that the average IQ is 100, while 140 is the beginning of genius IQ.

Facts- Sumerians, who lived in the Middle East, invented the wheel in about 3450BC. They also invented writing.

Facts- Karl Benz invented the first gas powered car with three wheels. The first car with four wheels was made in France in 1901 by Panhard et LeVassor.

Facts- Do you know that the first pick-up truck in the world was made by Gottlieb Daimler in 1886. Gottlieb produced the world's first motorcycle in 1885.

Fact- More than 60 million people annually visit France, a country of 60 million people.

Fact- Amazing! The only 15 letter word that can be spelled without repeating a letter is 'uncopyrightable'!

Facts- ENIAC was the name of world's first electronic computer. It was produced in 1946 and its size was humungous. Tech-savvy era!

Facts- Minnie Munro from Australia is the oldest bride to marry. She was a mere 102 years old when she married her boyfriend of 82 years.

Fact- Bookkeeper is the only word in English language with three consecutive double letters. Interesting!

Fact- The biggest plane in the world is the six-engined Antonov AN - 225 transport airplane. It can carry an aircraft on its back and cargo inside.

Fact- The word THEREIN contains 13 words spelt using consecutive letters- the, he, her, er, here, I, there, ere, rein, re, in, therein, and herein.

Facts- The famous Leonardo Da Vinci could write with one hand and draw with the other at the same time. Great talent!

Fact-Life on earth began about 3.5 billion years ago. The first life appeared in the sea. The sky was pink and the sea was rusty red.

Fact-It's amazing! The word 'Taxi' is spelt exactly the same way in English, French, German Swedish, Portuguese and Dutch.

Fact-It is estimated that millions of trees in the world are accidentally planted by squirrels that bury nuts and then forget where they hid them.

Fact-Galleons were trading & fighting ships that were used in the 15th & 16th century. The galleon mayflower took the 1st pilgrims to America in 1620.

Fact-Amazingly, pollen never deteriorates. It is one of the few natural substances that last indefinitely.

Fact- At the 1st world cup championship in Uruguay in 1930, the

soccer balls
that were used were actually monkey skulls wrapped in paper and
leather.

Fact- Amazing! People who lived during the Ice Age played musical
instruments. They made whistles out of bones and drums from
shoulder blades.

Fact-Amazing! Trial bikes can make short hops up almost vertical rock
faces. The rider needs good balance and expert control of the clutch
and gears.
Fact-Airport tugs pull aircrafts around when the aircraft cannot use its
engines. It has a tow bar that attaches to the aircraft front wheel.

Fact- GADFY, written by Earnest Wright in 1939 is a 50,000 + words
book, which
does not contain a single word with 'e' in it.

Fact- Experts say that one of the most alluring sleep distractions is the
24-hr
accessibility of the internet.

Fact-Engines on early motorbikes were not very powerful or reliable.
So the
bikes had pedals for going up-hill or in case there was a breakdown.
Fact- Each king in a deck of cards represents a king in history.
Spades-King
David, Clubs- Alexander, Hearts-Charlemagne & Diamonds-Julius
Ceasar.
Fact-During World war 1 a pigeon named Cher Ami saved the lives of
many French
soldiers by carrying a message across enemy lines amidst the battle.
Fact- Due to a retinal adaptation that reflects light back to the retina,
the
night vision of Tigers is six times better than humans.
Fact-Do you know? Lake Nicaragua in Nicaragua is the only fresh
water lake in the world that has sharks.
Fact-Do you know? It takes 110 domestic silkworm cocoons to make a

man's tie and 630 to make a woman's blouse.

Fact-Do you know? In relation to its overall size, the orangutan has the biggest arm span. Its arms are three times as long as its body.

Fact-Do you know, we humans are born with 300 bones in our body but as we grow older we are left with just 206!

Fact-Do you know that Sailor, Dead leaf, Paper kite, Blue stripped crow, Julia and Great Egg fly are all names of butterflies?

Fact-Do you know? A baby's eyes produce no tears until the baby is approximately six to eight weeks old. The tear glands are not formed till then.

Fact-Did you know? You can actually sharpen the blades on a pencil sharpener by wrapping your pencil in aluminum foil before inserting it.

Fact- Did you know? Ballpoint pens were invented by a Michigan scientist who was attempting to reduce the killing of birds for to their quills.

Fact-Did you know? A person afflicted with hexadectylism has six fingers or six toes on one or both hands and feet.

Fact- Did you know! Just like your fingers, your tongue has its own unique print which is different from any one else in this world.

Fact- Did you know that the Indian railway is the largest employer in the world? It employs over 1.6million people.

Fact-Did you ever notice, that the name of all the continents ends with the same letter that they start with.

Fact-Can you believe it? You will weigh less if you weigh yourself when the moon is full.

Fact-Believe it or not! The microwave was invented after a researcher walked by a radar tube and a chocolate bar melted in his pocket.

Fact-Believe it or not! No piece of normal-size paper can be folded into half more than 7 times.

Fact-Before the 1st humans went to space, animals paved the way. Laika, a Russian mongrel dog was the 1st earthling to have spent 7 days in space.

Fact-Basketball and rugby balls are made from synthetic material. Earlier, pigs' bladders were used as rugby balls.

Fact-Interestingly, in the 1880s, couples often rode side by side on tricycles (cycles with three wheels) called sociable's.

Fact-Interesting! An inventor in Tokyo has developed a laptop whose battery is recharged by the energy generated from the movement of the mouse.

Fact-In the early 1900s there were no gas stations. Village blacksmiths often kept a supply of gas to sell to car drivers whose tanks had run dry.

Fact-In Brazil there is an alternative source of fuel, taken directly from a plant. One Gas tree is able to produce nearly five gallons of fuel.

Fact-In 1949, American inventor Molt Taylor built a car which could be turned into a plane. By 1953, the car had flown over 25,000 miles.

Fact-In 1802 Andre Jacques Garnerin jumped from the basket of his hot-air balloon above London. It was the 1st successful parachute jump.

Fact-If you yelled for 8 years, seven months and six days, you would have produced enough sound energy to heat one cup of coffee.

Fact-Here's something you didn't know! The words in race car, Kayak' 7 radar' remain the same whether they are read left to right or right to left.

Fact-Hans Lippershey , a Dutch man who made spectacles, probably made the first telescope in 1608.

Fact-Cafe racers were specially modified bikes, which were raced to and from roadside cafes. This craze started in England in the 1960's.

Fact- Some fire trucks have telescopic ladders which are more than 130ft long when extended. Long enough to reach the 11th storey of a building.

Fact- Some cars are so fast that brakes alone aren't powerful enough to stop them. Parachutes drag these cars back to lower speeds.

Fact- Shockingly, even 24 Karat Gold is not pure gold; there is a small amount of copper in it. Pure gold is too soft to be moulded into a design.

Fact-Shocking! When Mahatma Gandhi died, an autopsy revealed five gold Kruger ands in his small intestine.

Fact- Replying to the same spam e-mail more than 100 times can overwhelm the sender's system & interfere with the ability to send any more spam.

Fact- Paraguay & Moldova are the only countries with national flags with different emblems on the obverse and reverse sides.

Fact- Modern race cars have wings! They are at the front & back of the car & are designed to prevent the car from taking off from the track.

Fact- Did you know that the word navy has been derived from the Sanskrit (the oldest language of the world) word 'Nou'.

Fact- Did you know that New Zealand is a home to 70 million sheep and only 40 million people.

Fact- Did you know that it is Joseph Swan who had invented the light bulb and not Thomas Edison!

Fact- When the first jet-powered plane took off on its maiden flight, it sucked a bird into its engine. The plane was the Heinkel He 178.

Fact – To prevent the passengers in the modern fast trains from falling, the computers in the train tilt it in the other direction while turning.

Fact- Forbidden City is one of the largest and best preserved palace complexes in the world today.

Fact- The common English name, the Forbidden City is a translation of the Chinese name Zinin cheng, which literally means Purple Forbidden City!

Fact- Eiffel Tower has three decks, the first two have restaurants and the top deck is a weather and communication platform with radio and TV antennae.

Fact- Alexandre Gustave Eiffel designed and built the Eiffel Tower. He built it for the world's Fair held in 1889.

Fact- More than 6 million visitors come to visit Eiffel Tower each year.

Fact- Queen Elizabeth 11 inaugurated the Sydney Opera House on October 20, 1973'.

Fact- Jorn Utzon designed the Sydney Opera House. He was a famous Danish architect and designer.

Fact- 60-65 million years ago, dolphins and humans shared a common ancestor.

Fact- US secret service sniffer dogs are put up in five-star hotels during overseas presidential visits.

Fact- In the eighteenth century the French Comte d'Artois owned a set of diamond buttons, each of which had a miniature clock encased inside it.

Fact- In the 1970's, the typical age range of people who gamble was 30-55. Today, it is age 17 – 70.

Fact- The states of Arizona and Hawaii have never adopted daylight savings time, neither has Puerto Rico, the virgin islands, or American Samoa.

Fact- 10 percent of all human beings ever born are alive at this very moment.

Fact- October 12th, 1999 was declared the day of six billion based on United Nations projections.

Fact- The cigarette lighter was invented before the match.

Fact- If Barbie were life-size, she would stand seven feet, two inches tall. Barbie's full name is Barbara Millicent Roberts.

Fact- In ancient Egypt, priests plucked every hair from their bodies, including their eyebrows and eyelashes.

Fact- The electric chair was invented by a dentist.

Fact-Average life span of a major league baseball: 7 pitches.

Fact- Ninety percent of New York City cabbies are recently arrived immigrants.

Fact- The first product to have a bar code was Wrigley's gum.

Fact- Did you know that Walt Disney was afraid of mice?

Fact- Surprisingly, pearls melt in vinegar.

Fact- The three most valuable brand names on earth: Marlboro, coca-cola and Budweiser, in that order.

Fact- It is possible to lead a cow upstairs but not downstairs.

Fact- The world's most expensive water is heavy water used as moderator in nuclear reactors.

Fact- Somewhere in the flicker of a badly tuned TV set is the background radiation from the Big Bang.

Fact-The earliest wine makers lived in Egypt around 2300 BC.

Fact- Ambulances were developed by Napoleon's surgeon in his Italian company of 1796-97.
Fact- A liter of vinegar is heavier in winter than in summer.

Fact- The highest recorded train speed is 320.2mph by the TGV train in France.

Fact- The highest speed ever achieved on a bicycle is 166.94 mph by Fred Rompelberg.
Fact- 85% of artificial Canada's trees are made in china. So are 80% of toys.
Fact - Are you aware of the fact that Wozniak sold his scientific calculator to raise capital?
Fact- Baking soda and vinegar will make your scrambled eggs fluffier.
Fact- Adcomsubordcomphibspac - is the longest acronym. A Navy term for Administrative Command, Amphibious Forces, Pacific Fleet Subordinate Command.
Fact- In the 1930's, America track star Jesse Owens used to race against horses and dogs to earn a living.
Fact- It took 10,000 workers & over 20yrs to build the Great Pyramid of Cheops, located outside Cairo, in Egypt. About 6.5 million tones of stone was used!

Fact- Lady Gaga wrote her new single 'Born This Way' in 10 minutes! Strange!
Fact- In the Middle Ages, chicken soup was believed to be an aphrodisiac.

Fact-Donald Duck comics were banned in Finland because the cartoon character doesn't wear pants.
Fact-Wyoming was the first state to allow women to vote.
Fact- When a lobster loses an eye it grows another one.
Fact- Were you aware of the fact the first baseball caps were made of straw? Strange!
Fact- There is exactly 46,783,665,034,756,288,456,012,645 move possibilities in a game of chess.
Fact- The world's tallest house of cards was over 25 feet tall.
Fact- The world's fattest cat weighs 22 pounds, making it Morbidly Obese!
Fact- University of Florida has an emergency plan in case of a sudden zombie attack.
Fact- The size of your foot is the distance from your wrist to your elbow.
Fact- The owner of the Segway company died as a result of riding a

Segway.

Fact- New York stock exchange started as coffee shop.

Fact- The can opener was invented 48years after the can.

Fact- If you stare at the numbers '63407113' long enough on a calculator you'll eventually see the word 'reactive'.

Fact- A badminton shuttle travels easily up to 180km/h (112 mph). It is one of the fastest objects in sports.

Fact- The most expensive video game ever developed was Shemue for Sega Dreamcast. It costs 20million dollars. Quite expensive you see!

Fact- The oil tanker Jahre Viking is the biggest ship ever built. It is 1504 feet long and 226 feet wide.

Fact- The original inspiration for Barbie dolls came from dolls developed by German propagandists in the late 1930s, with hints of Aryan features.

Fact- A fact about onion! It has no flavor, only a smell.

Fact- The poorest 40 percent of the world's population accounts for 5 percent of global income where as the richest 20 percent for 3-quaters.

Fact- The word Taxi is short for taximeter cab. A taximeter was a meter designed in 1891 that recorded the distance a horse-drawn cab had travelled.

Fact- Twenty-four emperors of the Ming and Qing dynasties lived in the Forbidden city.

Fact- Viswanathan Anand is India's first grandmaster. He became Grandmaster (GM) in 1988 at the age of eighteen. Hats off!

Fact - Want to go learn Chinese? Did you know that there are more than 40,000 characters in Chinese script?

Fact- Excavations from Egyptian tombs dating to 5,000 BC show that the ancient Egyptian kids played with toy hedgehogs.

Fact- An electric oven uses 1 kW-hr of electricity in 20mins, but 1 kW-hr may keep an electric clock ticking for 3 months. Incredible!

Fact- About 27% of food in developed countries is wasted each year. It's simply thrown away.

Fact- Since 1972, some 64 million tons of aluminum cans have been produced. These could get stretched to the moon about 1000 times.

Fact- Some trucks have armor plating on the outside. They are called armored personnel carriers (APC). They are used to carry troops on battlefields.

Fact- Surprising! When mechanical vehicles first appeared in Britain, a man had to walk in front of them carrying a red warning flag.

Fact- Amazing! An Australian mine train was weighed in 1996 at 72 ,191tons - that's more than eight Eiffel Towers!

Fact- Amazing! Bill Gates house was designed using a Macintosh computer which is a brand of Microsoft' rival company.

Fact- In a group of 23 people, at least two have the same birthday with the probability greater than 1/2.

Fact- In 1989, twenty-three people were hired in Jacksonville Florida just to flush toilets so the pipes would not freeze.

Fact- In 1975 Junko Tabei from Japan became the first woman to reach the top of Mount Everest.

Fact- In 1750 there were 800 million people in the world. In 1850 there were a billion more then, it took just 50 years to double to 6 billion.

Facts- From where did the air pollution started? It has started from the Industrial Revolution in Europe, which gradually became a major global problem.

Fact- US Post Office handles 43% of the world's mails. Its nearest competitor is Japan with 6%.

Fact - When the divorce rate goes up in the United States, toy makers report that the sales of toys also rise.

Fact – In Iceland, tipping at a restaurant is considered an insult! So, while making a trip there, be generous by your heart but not with money!

Fact- Were you aware that it was the Romans who made the first Popsicle. They took some ice and added flavour to it and then licked it. Yummy!

Fact- Surprising! Bees have 5 eyes. There are 3 small eyes on the top of a bees head and 2 larger ones in front.

Fact- Did you know that Children laugh about 400 times a day, while adults laugh on average only 15 times daily.

Fact- It's fascinating. The hair of an adult man or woman can stretch 25 percent of its length without breaking.

Fact- Canadian researchers have found that Einstein's brain was 15 percent wider than normal.

Fact- If you yelled for eight years, seven months and six days, you would have produced enough sound energy to heat one cup of coffee.

Fact- Did you know that there are no less than 717 native languages in a small country known as Papua New Guinea.

Fact- Were you aware that red wine gets spoilt if exposed to light; hence tinted bottles are used to store them.

Fact-Were you aware of the fact that the vocabulary of an average person consists of about 5,000 to 6,000 words.

Fact- New Jersey has a spoon museum that has over 5,400 spoons from across the world.

Fact- Can you believe it! When glass breaks, the cracks move at speeds of up to 3,000 miles per hour.

Fact- There are 293 ways to make change for a dollar. Oops, that's something interesting.

Fact- Do you know that next to man, the Porpoise is the most intelligent creature on earth?

Fact- In Greece, the climate is so warm that many of the cinemas do not have roofs.

Facts- Every noise in the world echo but a duck's quack does not echo. It is still an unresolved issue!

Fact- The bird that can fly the fastest is called White; it can fly up to 95 miles per hour.

Fact- Morihei Ueashiba, founder of Aikido, once pinned an opponent using only a single finger.

Fact- The world's youngest parents were 8 and 9 and lived in China in 1910.

Fact- Some of the deadliest land snakes live in Australia. A drop of their poison is sufficient enough to kill over 250,000 mice.

Fact- The cottonwood tree seed is surrounded by ultra-light, white fluff hairs that can carry it on the air for several days. Amazing!

Fact- When lightening strikes a sandy beach, the intense heat turns a small portion of the sand into glass, which are called 'fulgurites'.

Fact- Were you aware that a car uses 1.6 ounces of gas idling for 1 minute? Half an ounce is used to start the average automobile.

Fact- Did you know that Tulips are one of the fastest developing flowers. They can grow up to an inch a day after being cut.

Fact- The world's fastest reptile (measured on land) is the spiny-tailed iguana of Costa Rica. It has been clocked at 21.7mph.

Fact- The word four has four letters. In the English language, there is no other number whose number of letters is equal to its value. Amazing!

Facts- Amazing! Almost half the newspapers in the world are published in the United

States and Canada!

Fact- Did you know! The word Checkmate in chess comes from the Persian phrase Shah Mat, which means the King is dead.

Facts- The most expensive wedding cost over Euro 22 million and was held in a purpose built stadium in Dubai for a sheikh's son.

Facts- Did you know! The longest word in the English, as per the Oxford Dictionary is – pneumonoultramicroscopicsilicovolcanoconiosis.

Fact- Did you know the 1st toy balloon was made of vulcanized rubber!   It was thought of by someone in the J.G. Ingram Company in London in 1847.

Fact- Steve Fletcher holds the record for the largest gum wrapper collection. His collection has 5300 gum wrappers from all across the world.

Fact- 66percent of home based businesses are owned by women. This proves that women are smart!

Fact- We can produce laser light a million times brighter than sunshine.

Fact- Strange! The vampire bat has fewer teeth than the other bats as it doesn't chew its food. It basically lives on the blood of mammals.

Fact- The average lifespan of a cow is 7 years. The oldest cow ever recorded was Big Bertha. She reached 48 in 1993.

Fact- The interstellar gas cloud Sagittarius B contains a billion liters of alcohol.

Fact- Have you ever noticed that the king of hearts is the only king without a moustache on standard playing card?

Fact- Did you know that the glass produced from recycled glass instead of raw materials reduces related air pollution by 20, and water pollution by 50.

Facts- Surprising! Fingernails grow nearly 4 times faster than toenails.

Facts - About 3,000 years ago, most Egyptians died by the time they were 30!

Facts- Did you know that Neil Armstrong first put his left foot on the moon?

Health- The best way to avoid an itchy scalp is to wash hair using natural shampoos containing thyme, sage extract, zinc and other natural ingredients.

Facts- A snail can sleep for an average period of 3 years. Wow! Lucky chap eh?

Facts- Any clue about shortest complete sentence in the English language? Its, 'I am'.

Facts- Clever snake! Snakes can see through their eyelids even when their eyes are closed.

Facts- Who would you, think made the first wheelbarrow? It was first made by the Chinese.

Facts- Electricity doesn't move through a wire but through a field around the wire. Strange!

Facts- Sounds strange! But it's a fact that a violin contains about 70 separate pieces of wood!

Facts- It is believed that no piece of square dry paper can be folded more than 7 times in half!

Facts- Were you aware of the fact that Owls are one of the only birds who can see the colour blue?

Facts- In the White House, there are 13,092 knives, forks and spoons! Quite a huge number, isn't it?

Facts- In 1999, more than 5,000 teams competed in the second Bangkok league seven-a-side competition.

Fact- The largest snack ever eaten by a snake was an impala antelope. It was devoured by an African rock python which swallowed it without chewing.

Health- It is better to use gram flour instead of soap, to wash your face. This will leave you with a clear and shining complexion.

Fact- A cat sees about 6 times better than a human at night because of the tapetum lucidum, a layer of extra reflecting cells which absorb light.

Health- Berries contain anthocyanidins that are incredible antioxidants and have resveratrol, which helps fight heart disease and cancer.

Fact-Most cows give more milk when they listen to music. Seems, even cows need entertainment!

Fact- Men's shirts have the buttons on the right, but women's shirts have the buttons on the left. That's interesting!

Fact- In 1980, a Las Vegas hospital suspended workers for betting on when patients would die. Silly workers.

Fact- Can you imagine that in the year 1980, there was one country in the world with no telephones and it is Bhutan.

Fact- The filming of the movie Titanic cost more than the Titanic itself! Pretty expensive!

Fact- The energy of a discharge of an electric eel could start 50 cars. Let's keep one!

Fact- SNAILS have 14175 teeth laid along 135 rows on their tongue. How can they have so many teeth?

Fact- The banana tree cannot reproduce itself. It can be propagated only by the hand of man.

Fact- The average housewife walks 10 miles a day around the house doing her chores.

Fact- The average four year-old child asks over four hundred questions a day.

Fact-Surprising! Einstein could not speak fluently when he was nine. His parents thought he might be retarded.

Fact- A sneeze zooms out of your mouth at over 600 mph. Quite speedy, isn't it?

Fact- Bird droppings are the chief export of Nauru, an island nation in the western Pacific. Interesting business!

Fact- Did you know that Kotex was first manufactured as bandages, during the World War 1?

Fact- A huge underground river runs underneath the Nile, with six times more water than the river above.

Fact- Have you heard it before that if you leave a Goldfish in a dark room for years, it will turn white?

Fact- The starfish is one of the only animals who can turn its stomach inside-out and they also don't have brains!

Fact- A chicken who just lost its head can run the length of a football field before dropping dead. That's terrific!

Fact- A dogs scent membrane is about the size of a handkerchief. Its sensing lobe is also 4 times that of a human.

Fact- Do you know that the horse shoe crab has blue blood which can be used to kill bacteria. Quite a useful thing!

Fact - If you chew a cabbage/lettuce leaf properly, you will lose more energy than you will gain from actually eating it.

Fact- Have you ever noticed that Jack is the most common name in nursery rhymes? Quite amazing!

Fact- A whip makes a cracking sound because its tip moves faster than the speed of sound. Surprising!

Fact- Do you know that egg floats on water, in which sugar has been added! It's worth trying, isn't it?

Fact- There is 318,979,564,000 possible combinations of the first four moves in Chess!

Fact- Do you know that weevils are more resistant to poisons in the morning than at night?

Fact- Do you know that a dime (currency) has 118 ridges around the edge? Isn't it interesting?

Fact- Babies crawl an average of 200 meters a day! That's pretty much for the little ones!

Fact- Do you know that Whales die if their echo system fails. Strange!

Fact- The longest recorded flight of a chicken is 13 seconds! Amazing!

Fact- Iceland has the highest concentration of broadband users in the world.

Fact- Now that's an interesting fact! Married men tip better than unmarried men.

Fact- Do you know that men can read smaller prints than women; women can hear better?

Fact- There is more real lemon juice in Lemon pledge furniture polish than in country Time Lemonade.

Fact- When glass breaks, the cracks move faster than 3,000 miles per hour. That's really interesting!

Fact- Research indicates that mosquitoes are attracted to people who have recently eaten bananas.

Fact- The largest diamond ever found was an astounding 3,106 carats!

Health- If you are married, make time for intimacy in your relationship. It acts as a great stress reducer and keeps a marriage happy.

Fact- The reason honey is so easy to digest is that it's already been digested by a bee.

Fact- In medieval Thailand, they had moveable type printing presses. The type was made from baked oxen dung.

Fact- Sounds strange but it's true! The clocks that were made before 1687 had only one hand, and hour hand.

Fact-Isn't it surprising that the world's heaviest onion weighed more that the head of a man!

Fact- It's quite interesting to know that an average human move 25.4 times during sleep in a day!

Fact-Global Positioning System (GPS) is the only system today that can show your exact position on the Earth anytime, in any weather, no matter where you are!

Fact- The world's first University was established in Takshila, India in 700BC. More than 10,500 students from all over the world studied more than 60 subjects.

Fact- Can you believe it, that bone is five times stronger than steel! That's great!

Fact- Do you know that the first lady's boot was designed for Queen Victoria in 1840!

Fact- Do you know that Cotton, rags and paper take at least six months to break down?

Fact- Surprising! All the chemicals in a human body combined are worth about 6.25euro!

Fact- This is really interesting! You will not believe this one! A mosquito has 47 teeth.

Fact- Children between ages 6 to 10 exchange more than 650 million Valentine's cards with teachers, classmates, and family members. That's so cute!

Fact- A geep is the resulting offspring of a sheep and a goat.

Fact- 30 percent of Chinese adults live with their parents.

Fact- 44 percent of kids watch television before they go to sleep.

Fact- A jiffy is an actual unit of time for one 100th of a second.

Fact- A rat can fall from a five story building without injury.

Fact- A monkey was once convicted for smoking a cigarette in South Bend, Indiana.

Fact- Bruce Lee was so fast that they actually had to slow a film down so you could see his moves. Pretty quick man, he is!

Fact- Alexander Graham Bell, the inventor of the telephone, never telephoned his wife or mother because they were both deaf.

Fact- Do you know that due to a metal shortage during World War 11, Oscars were made of painted plaster for three years. Strange!

Fact- Every year around 1 billion Valentine cards are sent across. After Christmas it's a single largest seasonal card-sending occasion.

Fact- Do you know that the word set has the most number of definitions in the English language that is 192. Quite a meaningful word it is!

Fact- Did you know that blind people also dream. Their dreams don't have images but involve other senses such as sound, smell, touch and emotion.

Fact- You know what, chocolate consumption releases a chemical into your body very similar to what is produced when you are in love.

Fact- 90 percent of women who walk into a department store immediately turn to the right.

Fact- While human fingerprints are the means of our identification; the nose prints are the means of identifying Dogs!

Fact- Can you believe it, 315 entries in Webster's 1996 Dictionary were misspelled! That's not fair!

Fact- Tea was so expensive when it was first brought to Europe in the early 17th century that it was kept in locked wooden boxes.

Fact- The 1st Academy Awards (Oscars) were presented at a private dinner in the Hollywood Roosevelt Hotel, with less than 250 persons attending.

Fact- The average person's left hand does 56 percent of the typing.

Fact- Ancient Egyptians kissed with their noses instead of with their lips.

Fact- An average human speaks 4,800 words in 24 hours.

Fact- The smallest man ever was Gul Mohammed of India, who measured 1 feet, 10 inches.

Fact- The Mona Lisa has no eyebrows. It was the fashion in Renaissance Florence to shave them off.

Fact- The Nobel Peace Prize medal depicts three naked men with their hands on each others shoulders.

Fact- The longest regularly formed English word is

Praetertranssubstantiationalistically which contains 37 letters.

Fact- On an average, women blink nearly twice as much as men, and their heart beats faster than men's too.

Fact- The first known marketer of the flushing toilet was Thomas Crapper.

Fact- Traffic lights were used even before the invention of motor car.

Fact- Tug of war was an Olympic event between 1900 and 1920.

Fact- The world record for time without sleep is 264 hours – 11 days by Randy Gardner in 1965.

Fact- Tomatoes were once referred to as love apples. This is because there is a superstition that people would fall in love by eating them.

Fact- Lima beans contain cyanide.

Fact- Kite flying is a professional sport in Thailand.

Fact- Ketchup was sold in the 1830s as a medicine.

Fact- King Henry VIII slept with a gigantic axe.

Fact- Amazing! King George V of England owned a six-wheeled limousine. It was built by Crossley in 1929 and had a 3.8 litre, six cylinder engine.

Fact- The first plane to leave the ground was the steam-powered Eole. It was built by a French aviator, Clement Ader and had bat like wings.

Fact- The first human gender change took place in 1950 when Danish Dr Christian Hamburger operated on George Jargensen who became Christine.

Fact- The great surgeon Sushruta of ancient India (800BC), conducted complicated surgeries like artificial limbs, stones, plastic and brain surgery.

Fact- Amazing! Bill Gates house was designed using a Macintosh computer which is a brand of Microsoft's rival company.

Fact- The can opener was invented 48 years after cans were introduced.

Fact- The deepest mine in the world is Western Deep Levels near Charletonville, South Africa. It is 4.2km (2.6 miles) deep.

Fact- The harmonica is the world's best-selling music instrument.

Fact- The Major League Baseball teams use about 850,000 balls per season.

Fact- The oldest continuous trophy is the Americas Cup. It started in 1851 with Americans winning for 132 years until Aussies took it in 1983.

Fact- The only 2 animals that can see behind it's self without turning its head are the rabbit and the parrot.

Fact- The world's oldest surviving boat is a simple 3m long dugout dated to 7400 BC. It was discovered in Pesse Holland in the Netherlands.

Fact- Half the world's population earns about 5 percent of the world's wealth.

Fact- Do you know, the 17 year old, Junrey Balawing of Philippines, who is just 22 inches high, is the world's shortest man!

Fact- At just four years old, Mozart was able to learn a piece of music in half an hour.

5 ENVIRONMENTAL FACTS

Fact- Antarctica is the only continent without reptiles or snakes.

Fact- The great pyramid is the oldest structure in existence and is the sole remnant of the ancient Seven Wonders of the World.

Fact- All the planets in our solar system rotate anti clockwise, except Venus. It is the only planet that rotates clockwise.

Fact- Yuri Gagarin was the first person in space. He orbited the earth in a small capsule called Vostok with a journey lasting less than 2 hours.

Fact- Brooklyn Bridge is the largest suspension bridge in the world.

Fact- Exposure to diesel engine exhaust 'is associated with an increased risk for lung cancer' and possibly also for bladder cancer.

Fact- Hailstones are usually the size of peas but the biggest hailstorm was the
size of a watermelon. It fell in Kansas, USA in 1970.

Fact- The earth is magnetic. At the centre of the earth is a core of a molten
metal called iron, it is this that makes our planet a giant magnet.

Fact-Mars has 2 tiny moons, Deimos & Phobos, which look like potatoes! They might have been asteroids that Mars captured with its gravity.

Fact-Lightning doesn't happen before thunder. They happen at the same time, but you see lightning before you hear the thunder as light travels faster.

Fact-John Glenn went to space at the age of 77. Sensors on his skin were used to monitor his health. His flight happened 36yrs after his 1st space trip.

Fact-It takes 8 minutes for sunlight to travel from the sun to the earth!

This means, if you see the sun go out, it actually went out 8 minutes ago.

Fact- In the 14th century, Chinese merchants launched kites with people tied to them, to see if it was windy enough to set sail in their ships.

Fact-Mercury is the fastest planet. It zooms around the sun in just 88 days, at an incredible 107,000mph, faster than any space rocket.

Fact-Amazing! Mercury is the planet closest to the sun, but its neighbor Venus is even hotter, because it has clouds to trap in the heat.

Fact- An acre of trees can remove about tons of dust and gases every year from the surrounding environment. Let's all plant some trees!
Fact-An American Saturn 5' rockets were 364 feet tall monsters, weighing 2,903 tons on the launch pad. That's as heavy as 600 elephants!

Fact-Did you know? The amount of protein produced from a field of soya beans is 13 times greater than the same field used to graze cattle for meat.
Fact-Copernicus explained the seasons, by showing that the earth goes around the sun and also spins at the same time'.

Fact-By far the biggest ocean is the Pacific. It covers a 3rd of the earth. Between Panama and Malaysia it stretches about halfway around the world.
Fact-Astronauts are water-cooled! A system of tubes sewn into their space suits carries cool liquid around to keep their temperature normal.

Fact-If all the train tracks in America were laid end-to-end it could form a single track which would go almost 6 times around the world.

Fact-If all the coastal regions were straightened out, they'd stretch around the earth 13 times. At 55,800miles, Canada has the longest coast.

Fact-Some of Earth's oldest known rocks are found in Scotland. They are about 3.5billion years old.

Fact- Shockingly! While flying from London to New York via Concord, due to the time zones that are crossed, you can arrive 2 hours before you left.

Fact- Saturn is not only the planet with rings. Its rings are the easiest to see but Jupiter, Neptune and Uranus have them too.

Fact- Our galaxy has a twin. Andromeda is the biggest galaxy near the Milky Way. It's of the same age & a similar shape, but has many more stars.

Fact- Within a period of 10 minutes, a hurricane releases more energy than all the world's nuclear weapons combined.

Fact- When a baby iceberg breaks off a glacier, it is called 'calving'. Even smaller icebergs are called 'berg bits'.

Fact- The empire state building was designed from the top down by Gregory Johnson in just two weeks.

Fact- The empire state building cost a little more than 24,000,000 to build.

Fact- The empire state building has 6,500 windows.

Fact- It took 57,000 tonnes of steel to construct the steel skeleton.

Fact- Brooklyn Bridge was originally called the New York and Brooklyn Bridge. In 1915, it was formally named the Brooklyn Bridge.

Fact- Brooklyn Bridge is one of the oldest suspension bridges in the United States.

Fact- Brooklyn bridge is the first steel wire suspension bridge, and the first bridge to connect to Long Island.

Fact – The maximum seating capacity of the Opera theatre is 1,507 with 883 seats in the stalls, 466 seats in the dress circle and 158 seats in boxes.

Fact- Australian opera's production, war and peace, was the first opera performed in the Sydney opera house.

Fact- The weight of the Golden gate bridge, including the orthotropic re-decking carried out in 1986, is 380,800,000kg.

Fact- Golden Gate Bridge is illuminated by high-pressure sodium lights and with airway beacons on each tower.

Fact- Golden Gate Bridge has always been painted orange vermilion, better known as International orange.

Fact- Golden Gate Bridge was officially opened by President Franklin D. Roosevelt from the white house by pressing a telegraph key.

Fact- The biggest iceberg seen near Antarctica was almost the size of Belgium! The tallest iceberg was more than half as high as the Eiffel Tower.

Fact- The temperature on the surface of mercury exceeds 430 degree Celsius during the day, at night, plummets to minus 180 degrees centigrade.

Fact- The evaporation from a large oak or beech tree is from ten to twenty-five gallons in twenty-four hours.

Fact- The interstellar gas cloud Sagittarius B contains a billion litres of alcohol.

Fact- We can produce laser light a million times brighter than sunshine.

Fact- Ice does not melt when kept in liquid ammonia.

Fact- The grey whale migrates 12,500 miles from the Arctic to Mexico and back every year.

Fact- It would take over an hour for a heavy object to sink 6.7 miles down to the deepest part of the ocean.

Fact- The longest glacier in Antarctica, the Alembert glacier, is 250 miles long and 40 miles wide.

Fact- Antarctica is the only continent that does not have land areas below sea level.

Fact- It takes 8 minutes 17 seconds for light to travel from the suns surface to the earth.

Fact- The earth spins at 1,000mph but it travels through space at an incredible 67,000 mph.

Fact- In October 1999, an iceberg the size of London broke free from the Antarctic ice shelf.

Fact- The research spacecraft Helios B came within a record 27 million miles of the sun.

Fact- The highest recorded train speed is 320.2mph by the TGV train in France.

Fact- The international space station weighs about 500tons and is the same size as a football field.

Fact- Space debris travels through space at over 18,000mph.

Fact- The air at the summit of Mount Everest, 29,029 feet is only a third as thick as the air at sea level.

Fact- When a flea jumps, the rate of acceleration is 20 times that of the space shuttle during launch.

Fact- If you could drive your car straight up, you would arrive in space in just over an hour.

Fact- Every second 100 lightning bolts strike the earth.

Fact- Every year, over one million earthquakes shake the earth.

Fact- It is possible to see a rainbow as a complete circle from an aero plane.

Fact- The research spacecraft Helios B came within a record 27 million miles of the sun.

Fact- Astronauts brought back about 800 pounds of lunar rock to earth. Most of it has not been analyzed.

Fact- Englishman Roger Bacon invented the magnifying glass in 1250.

Fact- The oceans contain enough salt to cover all the continents to a depth of nearly 500 feet.

Fact- A typical hurricane produces the energy equivalent to 8000 one megaton bombs.

Fact- The risk of being struck by a falling meteorite for a human is one occurrence every 9,300yrs.

Fact-At over 2000 kilometers long, the Great Barrier Reef is the largest living structure on earth.

Fact- Chinas enormous Gobi Desert is the size of Peru and expanding 1400 square miles per year due to water source depletion and over-grazing.

Fact- America's fastest high speed train goes less than half as fast as the new train between Shanghai and Beijing (150mph vs 302 mph).

Fact-A thimbleful of a neutron star would weigh over 100 million tons.

Fact- If our sun were just an inch in diameter, the nearest star would be 445 miles away.

Fact-The deepest part of any ocean in the world is the Mariana trench in the pacific with a depth of 35,797 feet.

Fact- Neutron stars are so dense that a teaspoonful would weigh more than all the people on earth.

Fact- The largest meteorite craters in the world are in Sudbury, Canada, and in Vredefort, South Africa.

Fact- Saturn V rocket which carried man to the moon develops power equivalent to fifty 747 jumbo jets.

Fact- In olden days, sea captains kept pigs on board because they believed, should they be shipwrecked, pigs always swam towards the nearest shore.

Fact- Did you know, in the weightlessness of space a frozen pea will explode if
it comes in contact with an aerated drink?

Fact- The largest living thing on the face of this earth is an underground mushroom in Oregon. It measures three and a half miles in diameter.

Fact- The planet Saturn has a density lower than water. If there was a bath tub large enough to hold it, Saturn would float. Amazing!

Fact- The sky is shrinking & has been for 40yrs. About 5 miles of sky has been lost since 1958 & the figure may double over the next century.

Fact- There is three graded tones of paints every seven years to protect the Eiffel Tower from rust. It is painted in a brownish gray shade.

Fact- There is walls in space. Galaxies aren't evenly spaced through the Universe. They're arranged like walls around emptier regions of space.

Fact- There is so much water in the atmosphere, that if it all fell as rain, it would cover the entire surface of the earth to 2.5cm or 1 inch.

Fact- When a baby iceberg breaks off a glacier, it is called 'calving'. Even smaller icebergs are called 'bergy bits'.

Fact- When the weather is hot, some seals & sea lions flip tiny pebbles & sand onto their backs with their flippers to keep themselves cool.

Fact- John Glenn went to space at the age of 77. Sensors on his skin were used to monitor his health. His flight happened 36yrs after his 1st space trip.

Fact- Golf is the only sport played on the moon – on 6 February 1971; Alan Shepard hit a golf ball.

Fact- Due to earth's gravity it is impossible for mountains to be higher than 15,000 meters.

Fact- A compass does not point to the geographical North or South Pole, but to the magnetic poles.

Fact- The great pyramids used to be as white as snow because they were encased in a bright limestone that has worn off over the years.

Fact- The moon's gravity is much weaker than the earth's. This means, you would only weigh about one sixth of your earth-weight there.

Fact- In the 6th century BC, Greek mathematician Pythagoras said that earth is round - but few agreed with him.

Fact- In the 2nd century BC, Greek astronomer Erastosthenes accurately measured the distance around the earth is 40,000km but no one believed him.

Fact- Strange! An earthquake on December 16, 1811 caused parts of the Mississippi River to flow backwards!

Fact- Did you know! Mercury is the only planet whose orbit is coplanar with its equator.

Fact- The earth weighs around 6,600,000,000,000,000,000,000 tons (5,940 billion metric tons)!

Fact- Special fleece-like fabrics used in clothes and blankets can be made out of recycled plastic bottles. Strange!

Fact- The oceans contain enough salt to cover all the continents to a depth of nearly 500 feet.

Fact- We can produce laser light a million times brighter than sunshine.

Fact- Rain has never been recorded in some parts of the Atacama Desert in Chile. That's really strange!

Fact- Did you know that sunlight can penetrate clean ocean water to a depth of 240 feet?

Fact- Some large clouds store enough water for 500000 showers! Oops, that's surprising!

Fact- Sounds strange but true! The moon is one million times drier than the Gobi desert.

Fact- February 1865 is the only month in recorded history not to have a full moon! Strange!

Fact- Louisiana loses about 30 square miles of land each year to coastal erosion, hurricanes, other causes and a thing called subsidence, which means sinking.

Fact- The moon has mirrors on it. They were left there by astronauts who wanted to bounce laser beams off them, so that the distance to the moon can be measured.

Fact- Eighteen percent of all global carbon emissions are from cars. Main cause of global warming!

Fact- Everest is not the tallest mountain. Mauna Kea mountain in Hawaiian Island is 230m taller. It's 4,201m above water and 4,877m underwater.

Fact- The world's deadliest recorded earthquake occurred in 1557 in central China, more than 830,000 people were killed. Quite dangerous!

Fact- Do you know that a single day weather forecast requires about 10 billion math calculations! Quite a hectic job isn't it!

Fact- From a distance, Earth looks the brightest of the 9 planets. This is because sunlight is reflected by the planets water.

Fact- A fire in Australia has been burning for more than 5,000 years.

Fact- Quite interesting! Venice in Italy is built on 118 sea islets joined by 400 bridges. It is gradually sinking into the water.

Fact - Over 4 million cars in Brazil are now running on gasohol instead of petrol. Gasohol is a fuel made from sugar cane. Nice invention!

Fact- A car travelling 100mph would take more than 29 million years to reach the nearest star.

Fact- At least 300,000 people have been killed by volcanoes during the last 500 years. That's so scary!

Fact- Earth has over 12,000,000 species of animals, 3,000,000 species of plants and 1,000,000 other species.

Fact- An iceberg contains more heat than a lit match.

Fact- Austria was the first country to use postcards.

Fact- Australia has the greatest number of reptiles of any country in the world, with about 755 species.

Fact- Antarctica is the only land on our planet that is not owned by any country?

Fact- Jupiter is the fastest rotating planet, which can complete one revolution in less than ten hours.

Fact- The deepest mine in the world is the East Rams mine, which goes to a depth of about 3,585 metres.

Fact- The earliest maps were made by the Babylonians about 2300 B.C.

6 ANIMAL AND PLANT FACTS

Fact- Kiwis are the only birds, which hunt by sense of smell.

Fact- Chameleons can move their eyes independently. One eye can be looking forward and one eye backward at the same time.

Fact – Out of the 3,800 kinds of lizards, 2 are poisonous. They are the Gila
monster and the Mexican beaded lizard. They poison their victims after biting.
Fact- Geckos (a small to average sized lizard) have see-through eyelids. These
are clear flaps of skin which protect their eyes from dust & dirt.

Fact- Orb web spiders eat the old web before they spin a new one. A web may
take an hour to spin, but is as strong as steel of the same thickness.
Fact-Dinosaur eggs were only about 5 inches long. If they were any bigger, the
shell would have been too thick for the young to break through.
Fact- Surprising, dogs can't sweat! They don't have sweat glands. They pant
when they feel hot, to let the heat escape from their bodies.
Fact- Amazing! Grassland animals eat different bits of the grass to avoid
competition- Zebras eat the tops, wild beast eats the stems.
Fact- The biggest reptiles alive are saltwater crocodiles. They
are usually about 13 ft long but a gigantic crocodile killed in 1957 measured
about 28 ft.
Fact- The fastest sea mammal in the world is the killer whale.
With its streamlined body and powerful tail it can speed through the

water at up
to 35mph.

Fact- The snow leopard is a champ long jumper. It can cross a 5
foot wide ditch, that's over 1-1/2 times further than the human long-
jump
record.
Fact - Like ants and termites, honeybees live with thousands of
others in colonies. Honeybee nests very strong and can last up to 50
years.

Fact-Mako sharks are known to be incredibly fast swimmers with
superior lateral movements. They can reach the incredible speed of up
to 45mph.

Fact- Lories' are the most relaxed primates. Unlike their busy monkey
cousins, Lories' stroll very slowly through the forest in search of food.

Fact-Life in a zoo can make gorillas lazy & sometimes fat. The record
breaker was a male called N'gagi, who weighed in at a whopping 682
pounds.

Fact-Just before giving birth, a hippo isolates herself from the herd.
She stays isolated with the baby from 10-44 days before rejoining the
pack.

Fact-Jacanas are water birds that live in tropical places. Their very
long toes allow them to step on water plants without sinking.

Fact-It's surprising that, all birds comb or preen (groom), their feathers
with their beaks and claws. The cute 'love birds' preen each other.

Fact-It's shocking! At almost a quarter of a ton, the anaconda from
South America is the world's bulkiest snake.

Fact-It's fascinating, that bulls can run faster uphill than they can
downhill, because of the bone structure of their legs.

Fact-It's amazing! Crocodiles and alligators are very noisy. They
cough, hiss and roar to attract mates and keep in touch their group.

Fact-It's rude to look straight at a gorilla. In their language, starring means you're angry and looking for a fight. They beat their chest when crossed.

Fact-Ham (a chimp) was the 1st to try out the mercury capsule in 1961. Despite travelling at 5,000 mph, the chimpanzee survived the 16 min flight.

Fact- Termites build air conditioned mounds that can be up to 20ft tall. These
nets contain a maze of tunnels and can sustain millions of termites.
Fact- The biggest fish the whale shark is also harmless. This fish is 50 feet
long, weighs about 13 tons and swims slowly with the mouth wide open.
Fact- Sharks can sense their prey, even when there is no blood. A sensitive
lateral line along their bodies allows them to sense ripples in water.

Fact-Amazing! Urine from male cape water buffaloes is so flammable that some tribes use it for lantern fuel.
Fact- Amazing! Tortoises are real slow coaches. Most tortoises trudge along at speeds of less than 0.3mph, even when they're hungry.
Fact-Amazing! The water spider makes its home under the surface of the water. It waits inside until it spots its prey and then darts out.
Fact-Amazing! Orchids are grown from seeds that are so small that it would take thirty thousand of them to weigh as much as one grain of wheat.
Fact-Amazing! Lorises eat insects that are so toxic (poisonous) that they would give other animals a heart attack!
Fact- Amazing! Lizards love sunbathing. All reptiles are cold blooded. They can't control their own body temperature and rely on the weather instead.
Fact-Amazing! Leopard seals eat almost anything, including penguins, sea birds, fish, squid, seal pups and even duck-billed platypuses!
Fact-Amazing! Hyenas work as refuse collectors. Hyenas are scavengers-they will eat just about anything.
Fact- An ant's nest is made up of many chambers, connected by tunnels. Some rooms are nurseries, others are food cupboards and some are trash cans.

Fact-Amazingly, some whales have tones of tiny shellfish growing on their backs. These shellfish are called barnacles.

Fact-Amazing! Chimps take medicine. Chimpanzees sometimes eat plants that
don't taste very nice @ all, as cures for illness.

Fact-Amazing! Beetles and woodlice have an armor covering so tough that it is
difficult to crush. This protects them from their enemies.

Fact-Although we call them koala bears, koalas are really marsupials, which
means they have pouches like kangaroos. Pandas aren't bears either.

Fact-All young monkey's love to play and it's as important as school is for you!
This is how they learn the skills they will need when they grow up.

Fact-A shark's cornea can and has been used in an eye surgery, since its cornea
is similar to that of a human's.

Fact- A pelican has a beak with a stretchy pouch, which can hold far more fish
than its stomach! It scoops fish from water using its beak as fishing net.

Fact- A particular type of cobra spits poison on its enemy's faces! Spitting
cobras have very good aim. They can hit a target more than 6 fit away.

Fact- A little Gecko from Caribbean is the world's smallest lizard. This
reptile is just over an inch long, that's about as long as a human thumb.

Fact- A cheetah can run up to 76 kilometers per hour. That's really fast! The
fastest humans run @ about 37 kilometers per hour.

Fact- Amazing! Even meat eating bears sometimes like a change of diet! Polar
bears snack on seaweed and berries when seals are rare.

Fact-For more than 3,000 years, carpenter ants have been used to close wounds
in India, Asia and South America.

Fact-Do you know? Except for the African wild dog, all pet dogs have descended from a wolf-like ancestor, which appeared about one million years ago.

Fact-Dinosaur eggs were only about 5 inches long. If they were any bigger, the shell would have been too thick for the young to break through.

Fact-Did you know? Whales have a thick layer of fat called blubber, under their skins. This is what keeps them warm in the cold sea.

Fact-Did you know? That rat multiplies so quickly that within a span of 18 months, two rats could have over a million descendants.

Fact-Did u know! The fastest land snakes are the deadly black mambas. These speedy snakes can race along at about 12mph.

Fact- Did you know! Many primates, including baboons, who spend a lot of time sitting around, have built-in padding on their backsides.

Fact-Did you know that eagles can catch animals much bigger and heavier than themselves. The harpy eagle from South America is the biggest of all.

Fact-Cookie cutter sharks are often happy with just a bite or two from their prey. The wounds they make are oval-shaped, a bit like a cookie.

Fact- Click beetles lie on their backs as if they were dead to fool their enemies. They then suddenly spring up in the air, twist and run away.

Fact-Chimpanzees who live on mount Tai, in West Africa, use a stone as a nutcracker to smash open the hard shells of the cola nut.

Fact-Cheetah mothers don't have permanent dens. They move their cubs around a couple of times each week. This prevents others from preying on them.

Fact-Can you believe it! Monkeys do sentry duty. When their troop is enjoying a feast, one or two monkeys keep a lookout for predators.

Fact-Can you believe it! Camels' milk which is widely drank in the Arabian countries, has 10 times more iron than cow's milk.

Fact-Big sea birds glide on air currents, sometimes not landing for months. Swifts can spend years in the air, only landing to nest and mate.

Fact-@ about 4 inches long, thread snakes are the shortest and thinnest snakes in the world. They could slither through the lead hole of a pencil.

Fact-@ a top speed of about 18.77m/s the greyhound is not only the fastest dog but second only to the Cheetah as the world's fastest animal.

Fact-Armies transport equipment in amphibious trucks that can drive on land like a normal truck and float across water like a boat.

Fact-An owl is the only bird that drops its upper eyelids to blink. All other birds raise their lower eyelids.

Fact-In the Jurassic age, giant plant eaters called sauropods became the largest animals on earth. One of them was as tall as 6 storey building.

Fact-Humpback whales are very athletic. Despite the weight, they can leap high into the air & come crashing down into the water on their backs.

Fact-Humming birds are the smallest birds in the world. The bee humming bird of Cuba is as big as a bumble bee & can flap at up to 90 beats/sec.

Fact-Humming birds are special. They can fly forwards, sideways, backwards and can remain in a spot by flapping their wings very quickly.

Fact-Horned dinosaur's centrosaurus lived in large groups like elephants. When threatened, the adults surrounded the young, making a wall of horns.

Fact-Some sea mammals can hold their breath for almost 2 hours before coming to the surface for air. Most humans can only hold it for a min or so.

Fact-Some of the deadliest land snakes live in Australia. A drop of their poison is sufficient enough to kill over 250,000 mice.

Fact-Some nests are huge. An eagle's nest or eyrie is so big that you could lie down in it. Some birds like the hummingbirds make tiny nests.

Fact-Some large submarines and some aircraft carriers have nuclear powered engines. They can travel for several months without having to re-fuel.

Fact-Snakes don't smell things with their nose; they pick up smell with their tongue which they flick in and out.

Fact- Snakes can't hear at all. They have no ears for detecting sound. Instead they pick up vibrations in the ground through their bodies.

Fact- Snake charmers make it seems as if a snake is dancing to music but the snake follows the movement of charmer's pipe with its eyes, ready to attack.

Fact-Shockingly, Chimpanzees have a special fear grin. They use it to warn others of danger without making a giveaway noise.

Fact- Shield bugs protect their eggs from hungry predators by sitting on them & after hatching they look after their young till they can move.

Fact- Sharks get very excited at the smell of blood. They can smell a drop of blood, diluted millions of times, half a mile away.

Fact- Sharks can sense their prey, even when there is no blood. A sensitive lateral line along their bodies allows them to sense ripples in water.

Fact- Mega Odon, a prehistoric shark was the apex predator with an average size of 12-18 meters.

Fact- Sharks apparently are the only animals that never get sick. As much as is known, they are immune to every known disease including cancer.

Fact- Shark skin is very tough, with teeth like dentils. Therefore shark skin was once used for smoothing down wood, instead of sandpaper.

Fact- Seals sometimes look as if they're crying, but it's not because they are sad. The tears keep their eyes moist and clean.

Fact- Pigs cannot sweat because they don't have sweat glands. Instead, they roll around in mud to keep themselves cool.

Fact- Paper wasps build nests out of thin sheets of paper. They make the paper themselves by scraping wood with their jaws & mixing it with saliva.

Fact-Moths are unable to fly during an earthquake.

Fact- When hippos get upset their sweat turns red.

Fact- Young dragonflies live in ponds and streams. They catch tadpoles and small fish using a special lower lip, which shoots out to stab and hold prey'.

Fact – When born, a baby gibbon has a cap of fur on the top of its head and just like human babies; the rest of the body is completely bare.

Fact- Weighing approximately 6 kg at birth, a baby caribou (reindeer) doubles its weight in just 10 days.

Fact- Unlike spiders, insects and other creepy-crawlies, scorpions give birth to live young ones. The mother carries all her children on her back.

Fact- Tortoises have the longest life span amongst all animals. The oldest tortoise was Marion's tortoise from Seychelles who died at the age of 150 in 1918.

Fact- To scare rivals, a male hooded seal blows air into its nose. This inflates the lining of 1 of its nostrils and it looks like a big red balloon.

Fact- To make 1 kilo of honey, bees have to visit 4 million flowers, travelling a distance which equals to going 4 times around the earth.

Fact- Tiny plants that live in the sea, called planktons, produce nearly three quarters of the earth's oxygen.

Fact- Heart of a blue whale beats only nine times per minute.

Fact- The average cow spends 13 hours a day lying down.

Fact- Roosters cannot crow till they extend their necks.

Fact- The smallest monkey is the Pygmy Marmoset; an adult weighs a little more than 3 ounces and is 5 inches long with an 8 inch tail.

Fact- The scales of a crocodile are made of keratin, the same substance that hooves (animal feet) and fingernails are made of.

Fact- The pre-historic Woolly mammoths were big elephants with extra –long tusks up to 10 feet long.

Fact- Surprising! Plant-eater dinosaur's swallowed stone called gastrulates, to help grind down tough plant food inside their stomachs.

Fact- The flea can jump 350 times its body length. It's like a human jumping the length of a football field.

Fact- A cockroach will live nine days without its head, before it starves to death.

Fact- The biggest reptiles alive today are saltwater crocodiles. They are usually about 13ft long. A gigantic crocodile killed in 1957 was up to 28 ft.

Fact- The male praying mantis cannot copulate while its head is attached to its body.

Fact- A single rye plant can spread up to 400 miles of roots underground.

Fact- Polar Bears are nearly undetectable by infrared cameras, due to their transparent fur.

Fact- Polar Bears can run @ 25 miles an hour and jump over 6 feet in the air.

Fact- The world's smallest winged insect, the Tanzanian parasitic wasp, is smaller than the eye of a housefly.

Fact-A salmon-rich, low cholesterol diet means that Inuit's rarely suffer from heart disease.

Fact- The low frequency call of the humpback whale is the loudest noise made by a living creature.

Fact- Chickens can't swallow while they are upside down.

Fact- In a fight between a polar bear and a lion, the polar bear would win.

Fact- The smartest dogs are the Jack Russell terrier and Scottish Border collie.

Fact- The giraffe has the highest blood pressure of any animal.

Fact- Just one cow gives off enough harmful methane gas in a single day to fill around 400 litre bottles.

Fact- The average garden-variety caterpillar has 248 muscles in its head.

Fact- The shell of an egg constitutes 12 percent of an egg's weight.

Fact- The call of the humpback whale is louder than Concorde and can be heard from 500 miles away.

Fact- A group of ravens is called a murder.

Fact- The poison arrow frog has enough poison to kill 2,200 people.

Fact- Penguins are the only bird that can leap into the air like porpoises.

Fact- A crocodile cannot stick its tongue out.

Fact-Oak trees do not produce acorns until they are fifty years of age or older.

Fact- Donkey's kill more people annually than plane crashes.

Fact- Strange but true! Butterflies taste with their feet.

Fact- A duck's quack does not echo and no one knows why.

Fact- Turtles can breathe through their butts.

Fact- Quasars emit more energy than 100 giant galaxies.

Fact- Chimpanzees are very clever! They can understand 300 different signs.
Fact-Female black widow spiders eat their males after mating.
Fact-The dinosaurs became extinct before the Rockies or the Alps were formed.
Fact- The combined length of the roots of a Finnish pine tree is over 30 miles.
Fact- The short-nosed Bandicoot has a gestation period of only 12 days.
Fact-The dinosaurs became extinct before the Rockies or the Alps were formed.
Fact- Bats always turn left when exiting a cave.
Fact- When hippos get upset their sweat turns red.
Fact- Large kangaroos can cover more than 30 feet with each jump.
Fact- A sun dew plant uses the sticky liquid on its leaves to trap insects. It uses the hair on its leaves to hold the insects.
Fact- Did you know that birds only use nests for laying eggs and raising their chick? They rest at night in the hedges, trees or holes.
Fact- Venezuelan brown bat can detect & dodge individual raindrops in mid-flight, arriving safely back at his cave completely dry.
Fact- Mice never get more than 29ft. from the place they are born.

Health- The best Gas (flatulence) home remedy is to have a pinch of asaefotida with a pinch of rock salt for quick relief.

Fact- Hershey's kisses are called that because the machine that makes them looks like as if it's kissing the conveyor belt!

Health -To get rid of stones in the kidneys or gal-bladder, have celery as food. Its regular intake prevents future stone formation.

Fact- A chameleons tongue is twice the length of its body.

Fact- The African ostrich can grow over 8 feet tall, which is much taller than the average man.

Fact- The American turkey vulture helps human engineers detect cracked or broken underground fuel pipes. Quite an intelligent bird, isn't it?

Health- Kelp Sea weed is an excellent home remedy for typhoid, its antioxidant property and iodine presence would assist thyroid function.

Fact- The Basilisk lizard escapes from its enemies by running across the water. It runs so fast on its long fringed back toes that it doesn't sink.

Health- Two teaspoons apple cider vinegar and 2-3 teaspoons of honey dissolved in a small glass of warm water gives relief from joint pains.

Fact- The biggest fish the whale shark is also harmless. This fish is 50 feet long, weighs about 13 tons and swims slowly with the mouth wide open.

Fact- The biggest pig in recorded history was Big Boy of Black Mountain, North Carolina, which was weighed 1,904 pounds in 1939.

Fact- The tomato is the world's most popular fruit and just like the brinjal and the pumpkin, botanically speaking it is a fruit, not a vegetable.

Fact- Were you aware of the fact that only one out of a thousand baby sea turtles survive after hatching.

Fact- Amazing! A jellyfish is 95 percent water.

Fact- A snail can have about 25,000 teeth.

Fact- A rodent's teeth never stop growing.

Fact- A queen bee lays 1500 eggs a day.

Fact- A dog's sweat glands are found between their toes.

Health- Application of Aloe Vera gel or Vitamin E has the benefits to cure stretch marks.

Fact- A rat can go without water longer than a camel.

Fact- A shark can grow a new set of teeth in a week.

Fact- A Koala Bear sleeps 22 hours of every day.

Fact- A hippopotamus can run faster than a man.

Fact- A dragonfly has a life span of 24 hours.

Fact- Crocodile is the only animal and reptile that sheds tears while eating.

Facts- Chained Dogs are 3 times more likely to bite than unchained dogs.

Fact- Chewing gum while peeling onions will reduce your tears.

Fact- Black pepper is the most popular spice in the world.

Fact- An owl has three eyelids.

Fact- Bananas grow pointing upwards.

Fact- An oyster can change its gender.

Fact- Cats urine glows under a black light.

Fact- Almonds are a member of the peach family.

Fact- An ostrich's eye is bigger than its brain.

Facts- An elephant can smell water three miles away.

Fact- An elephants tooth can weigh as much as 5kgs.

Fact- Despite the hump, a camel's spine is straight.

Fact- An elephant trunk has no bones but 40,000 muscles.

Fact- The longest snake is the King Cobra, which can rear itself up to six feet and spread its hood nine inches.

Facts- The largest earthworm on record was found in South Africa and measured 22 feet.

Fact- Cows release some 100 million tons of hydrocarbon annually-by releasing gas.

Fact- Lions cannot roar until they reach the age of two.

Fact- Lobsters have blue blood.

Fact- Armadillos, the mammal have four babies of the same sex, at a time. They are perfect identical quadruplets. Interesting!

Fact- Are you aware of the fact that Rhinoceross horn is made of the same material, which is found in our hair and fingernails, called keratin?

Fact- Wolffia blooms are the smallest flowers. The size is so small that even a bouquet of a dozen would comfortably fit on the head of a pin.

ABOUT THE AUTHOR

Okechukwu Martins Onuoha is a Librarian by profession. He enjoys learning, and spends time daily blogging @ www.okeymartins.blogspot.com , reading, watching football and exercising. Martins is married to Prisca C. Martins with whom he has 2 daughters: Somto and Genevieve. He is a graduate of 'Safety Manager', Oshacademy, USA and has a Diploma in 'Food Safety', Alison, Ireland. He is a brother too with 4 sisters and 3 brothers. Martins has so many first cousins. He is a former United Nations Volunteer Intl. In his free time, reading, watching football matches, walking and playing football are Martins's pastimes. Martins has published books titled - Stop Smoking Now, Communications Break-Down. Actual Facts And Figures is his third book and he looks forward to writing many more books that will be published.

www.ingramcontent.com/pod-product-compliance
Lightning Source LLC
Chambersburg PA
CBHW070359290526
45790CB00004B/1557